INTRODUCTION

I did it again. Without first initiating my brain, I opened my mouth and spewed out something stupid. I'm totally embarrassed. Others are hurt.

I wish I could get an instant Mouth Makeover. How relieved I would be if I could find some simple way to prevent mouth mishaps from happening. If only I could call up a Magic Makeup Lady to fix my problem!

"Hello, this is Luscious Lips, Incorporated. How may I help you?"

"Oh, thank goodness you're there! I'm in desperate need of a Mouth Makeover!"

"Oh dear, that does sound serious. Tell me exactly, what is the problem?"

"Well, I hate to admit it, but every time I open my mouth, tactless and thoughtless words seem to come out!"

"Now, calm down. I'm quite sure I can find a solution. In order to offer you our best advice, I need to ask a few more questions. So, what brand of lipstick are you using on your lips right now?"

"That's easy! The brand I've been using lately is Loud and Lauder."

"Ah yes, that is a popular brand. Can you tell me which colors have you been wearing?"

"Let me get out my makeup bag and check. Let's see. Here are two of my favorites—Insensitive Iris and Hurtful Hyacinth. And this one I wear all the time—it's called—oh, Foot-in-Mouth Fuchsia!"

"Well, I think we may have found the problem. Fortunately, this is an easy fix. First, I recommend our best lip exfoliator to scrub off any residue from your previous lipsticks and then daily use of our number one product, Perfection Pink. I can send those right out to you and that should take care of the problem!"

If only fixing my mouth were as easy as ordering a new tube of lipstick. My days of putting my foot in my mouth would be over. No longer would I have to taste sock lint or shoe leather.

I have wished for a Mouth Makeover for a long time. When I was young, I wished I was like the girls who were the life of the party—the ones who talked easily while I sat tongue-tied in the corner. Later, I admired the caring, empathetic ladies in my life—the women everyone in my circle of friends went to for advice. Then I admired the moms who seemed to never lose their patience—the mothers who always had a pearl of wisdom for their children.

If there were a Magic Makeup Lady, I would ask her for the product that would enable me to tell a joke without forgetting the punch line. I would purchase the lipstick that would enable me to say just the right thing at just the right time. I would pay dearly for the lip gloss that would prevent me from yelling at my kids or nagging at my husband.

I want to be like my sister-in-law, Kathy, who is gifted at making everyone feel important by asking insightful questions that bring out the best in people. I want to be like my friend Linda, who never fails to make me feel good about myself. I want to be like my sister, Shelly, who always makes me laugh.

But most of all, I yearn to emulate Christ, who gave words of wisdom. I aspire to imitate the Savior who shared comfort and encouragement, forgiveness and peace. I desire to be like Jesus who offered grace.

Although it would be nice to be the life of the party and always know the right thing to say, the real reason I want to transform my speech, the reason I think it is worth the effort, is because Jesus thinks it's important. Recently, I read through the Bible and wrote down all the passages I could find that dealt with speech. I was amazed at how many times God talks about our words. Did you know that the Book of Proverbs alone has 108 verses dealing with our mouths, lips, and tongues? Our heavenly Father is encouraging all of us to begin a Mouth Makeover!

Not long ago, I went to a cosmetics expert at a department store and asked for a literal Mouth Makeover. Patty, my makeup artist for the day, first used an exfoliator that softened my lips by removing dead skin and rough spots. Then she used a product that moisturized, repaired, and plumped my lips. The next step in my Mouth Makeover was a lip liner used to define my lips and to help the lipstick adhere. Patty followed that with a long-lasting lip color in a gorgeous neutral color. Finally, she added a dab of sparkly lip gloss in the middle of my lips to add a bit more shine.

If I had wanted to, I also could have purchased lip balm, lip primer, and lip sealer.

Who knew it took so many products to achieve the perfect pout?

Ultimately, most of us will not be willing to spend that much time and money on fancy lip products that will have only a temporary effect on our beauty. Probably some of us prefer not to fuss with makeup at all!

However, when we go to our Heavenly Makeup Artist, He will assist us with a true Mouth Makeover. He can help us use a spiritual version of an exfoliator to scrub off our negative words. He can teach us to use a soothing lip balm that will help us to spread encouragement. His Word, like a fully stocked cosmetics bag, has all the tools necessary to beautify our lips with praise and truthful witness.

Now I can't tell you that using these tools will enable you to have a flawless mouth and that you will never say another rotten thing in your life. There is no Perfection Pink available here on earth. But we can receive God's grace and become more consistent in wearing Complimenting Coral, Revitalizing Red, and Praising Peony.

But I can tell you that this Mouth Makeover is worth the effort because transforming our words can improve our relationships. Changing what comes across our lips will affect our attitude toward life. And most important, altering our tongues' response will enrich our connection to God as we spend more time in prayer and praise.

In each session of this study, we tackle a different step in developing godly speech. Each chapter has reading material and a study guide. The readings include an examination of what the Bible has to say about our words and some practical steps to take toward a Mouth Makeover. I encourage you to write in your copy of this book. Underline or highlight passages that inspire or challenge you. Make notes in the margins. Write questions about things that are unclear or that you want to discuss with your pastor or members of your group. The study guide will help you to discover additional Bible passages on the topic and to apply these truths to your life.

There are a few tools consistently used throughout the book:

What key lesson did you learn today? Each day you will be asked this question. Your answer can be from the reading, from the Bible passages examined, or from a thought that God revealed during your time with Him. Answering this question will help you to choose one idea or concept to inspire your day.

Memory verse: You will be instructed daily to write out the memory verse for the week. The act of writing out the words of Scripture will help you to commit them to heart. You might also write the verse on a card to carry in your purse or on a sticky note to display by the sink, mirror, or computer monitor. Storing God's Word in our hearts is one of the most effective ways of changing our habits.

Meaningful Makeover: The Bible is full of fascinating people, amazing stories, and thought-provoking quotes, but if that is all we get out of it, then we have missed the point. The Bible is God speaking to us, instructing us, and guiding us. The Meaningful Makeover section will help you to apply God's Word to your life. Each day this section will ask you to focus on one aspect of your speech and evaluate your progress. There is space available to journal your reactions or prayers.

LIP Study: On the fifth day of every week, we will examine more deeply one section of Scripture using a three-step process following the acronym LIP:

Look for the Facts

Interpret the Meaning

Pursue the Application

Allow a little more time to complete your study on this day. Using this three-step process will enable you to discover details in God's Word. It will help you take time to hear Him speak to your heart. If you are doing the study in a group, you might talk about the process. Or perhaps have each person share the lessons she learned that week doing this exercise. I hope that you will find the LIP technique helpful.

We don't need a Magic Makeup Lady to accomplish a Mouth Makeover. We don't have to spend a fortune to find the right color for our lips. Our heavenly Father has all we need to have the perfect shade of speech. His Word and His Spirit will provide everything required to develop lovely, God-pleasing lips.

Exfoliate: Scrub with Forgiveness

Memory Verse

*Let the words of my mouth and the meditation of my heart be acceptable in Your sight, O L*ORD*, my rock and my redeemer.*
Psalm 19:14

STEP 1

Do You Need a Mouth Makeover?

For we all stumble in many ways. And if anyone does not stumble in what he says, he is a perfect man, able also to bridle his whole body. James 3:2

One hectic Saturday, I was driving along a busy road, trying to keep up with traffic and paying attention to the cars around me, when the traffic light turned red and I found myself stopped behind Marty's Handyman Service van. While I waited for the light to turn green, I read Marty's slogan: "I can fix what your husband repaired."

My husband, John, is a fix-it genius, but I laughed out loud when I read those words because I have heard many stories of people who paid more for a repair after they tried a do-it-yourself project than they would have paid had they hired a professional in the first place.

As I contemplated Marty's ad, I found myself thinking how wonderful it would be if I could hire a service to fix what my mouth has done. There have been many occasions when I would have jumped at the chance to use a business that promised "I can fix what you wish you hadn't said."

One such occasion happened when I was about twenty years old. I was talking to a friend I had not seen in a while. A mutual friend had reported months ago that he and his wife were expecting a child, so I asked if they had brought the baby to the gathering.

"No," my friend answered, "it turned out to be a false pregnancy."

"False pregnancy?" I queried.

"Yes, she had all the symptoms, but was not actually carrying a child."

I should have expressed my condolences, but for some reason what came out of my mouth was: "Oh, we thought you would have had the baby by now!"

His face fell, and he softly said, "So did we." At that point, my mind fully registered that what I had said was insensitive and I promptly apologized. But the damage was done.

If I had thought before I had spoken, I probably would have realized that their loss was real, their heartache painful. How I wished that I could take back my words that caused the look of anguish on my friend's face. If only I could call up Marty's Handyman Service and say, "My mouth has messed up again. Can you come and fix the damage?"

Can you relate? Wouldn't it be nice if we could hire a service to take care of our mouth messes? Or even better, wouldn't it be terrific if we could call up a Magical Makeup Lady to purchase a new tube of lipstick that would give us the perfect Mouth Makeover? Wouldn't it be wonderful if applying the right shade of lip gloss would prevent our lips from spouting lies, gossip, and hurtful words?

Every day, I choose to wear lipstick, lip stain, or lip gloss on my lips. Some of my favorite shades are natural blush, pink kiss, and coral silk. I opt for a product that moisturizes my lips and a color that brightens my face.

Did You Know?

- In the U.S. hundreds of millions of dollars are spent on lipstick each year.
- 75–85 percent of American women wear this product.
- Lipstick consistently outsells other cosmetics by a wide margin.
- Clinique sells a tube of lipstick every second.[1]

Each day, I also have a choice in my speech. I start out the day with great intent to wear the shades of speech that will soothe my family and cheer up my friends. But sometimes I inadvertently choose colors that not only fail to brighten my face, but darken others' faces as well. It is then I realize my need for a Mouth Makeover.

Unfortunately, a Mouth Makeover is not as easy as going to the cosmetics counter and buying a new lipstick. I can't purchase a tube of Perfection Pink that will block all my angry outbursts, careless speech, and hurtful words. A Mouth Makeover that will change my words begins with God. He has a plan to transform my lips.

The first step in our Mouth Makeover is to exfoliate. A makeup expert will tell you that before you put lipstick on your lips, you must first slough off the dead skin. She will help you choose an exfoliating product that will ensure a smooth palette for a lovely, rich color.

A Prayer for a Mouth Makeover

Use Psalm 19:14 as a prayer to begin your Mouth Makeover:

May every utterance and every word that comes out of my mouth and every musing and thought of my heart bring You pleasure and delight, O LORD. Let me always speak as if I were in Your presence for truly You are always with me. Help me to remember You are my Redeemer—the One who saved me and who will continue to forgive me when I fail. Help me recall that You are my Rock—the source of my strength. Psalm 19:14 (Sharla Fritz amplified version)

God also wants to do some exfoliating in our lives. He wants to scrub off the effects of any negative words we may have spoken and receive His word of forgiveness. This week, He will help us to recognize our messy mouth and will launder our lips. We will receive a new chance to speak words of encouragement, praise, and thanksgiving. And God will help us to recognize the power we have in a telling tongue.

A Word of Forgiveness for Today

Christ my Redeemer, forgives me when I fail. He is my source of strength in my Mouth Makeover.

Makeup experts tell us if we are going to wear only a single cosmetic, lipstick is the one that can transform our faces and the way we feel about ourselves. Sporting a new shade of speech may not give us a cover girl look, but it can transform our relationships, change our self-image, reflect a Christlike attitude, and most important, please our Savior.

Father in heaven, it is my desire that my words would bring You pleasure and delight. Too often I make a mess of things. I know that it will take some work on my part and a reliance on Your grace to change the shade of speech I wear. Help me to experience a Mouth Makeover. Thank You for Your work in my heart and mouth. In Jesus' name. Amen.

DAY 1

Lipstick Lesson

1. How is the lipstick you put on your mouth similar to the words that come out of it? How is it different?

2. Our memory verse this week is Psalm 19:14: "Let the words of my mouth and the meditation of my heart be acceptable in Your sight, O Lord, my rock and my redeemer." Let's examine each phrase in this verse to bring more meaning to it.

   a. "Let the words of my mouth and the meditation of my heart" What do the following passages say about the connection between our mouths and our hearts?
   Proverbs 16:23:

   Matthew 12:33–37:

   b. "Be acceptable in Your sight, O Lord" How do we become acceptable in God's sight?
   Romans 3:23–24:

   Ephesians 2:8:

   c. "My rock and my redeemer" The following verses talk about God as a rock and a redeemer. What characteristics of God do you see in these passages? How can these characteristics assist us in a Mouth Makeover?
   Psalm 18:1–2:

   Psalm 103:2–4:

3. What key lesson did you learn today?

4. Our memory verse for this week is Psalm 19:14, "Let the words of my mouth and the meditation of my heart be acceptable in Your sight, O LORD, my rock and my redeemer." To help you memorize this verse, write the words here in your own handwriting. You might also want to post the verse in conspicuous spots like your mirror, computer, or fridge.

Meaningful Makeover

Pray to God the words of our memory verse. Ask Him to help you be aware of your speech today. Pray that your words will be pleasing to Him and valuable to others. At the end of the day or the start of the next day, evaluate your words and use the space below to journal about what came out of your mouth. This is not meant to be condemning, but simply to make you more attentive to what comes out of your mouth.

Messy Mouth

Woe to me! For I am lost; for I am a man of unclean lips, and I dwell in the midst of a people of unclean lips; for my eyes have seen the King, the LORD of hosts! Isaiah 6:5

When I was pregnant with Anna, my first child, I read many books about child-rearing. I wanted to do all the right things and speak all the correct phrases. Before Anna was born, I had delusions that I could be the perfect parent.

One of the things I vowed I would never say was "Because I said so!" All the parenting books I read instructed me to reason with my child and explain my rules and directions. I didn't want to demand obedience from my daughter without logic and motivation.

I was able to keep this resolution until one day when I now had two small children demanding my time and attention. They were in the family room and their squabbling swelled while my tolerance shriveled. When I couldn't stand the noise any longer, I shouted above the din, "Quiet down!" One of them (probably the three-year-old) asked "Why?"

I shouted again, "Because I said so!"

Even as the words flew out of my mouth, I realized what I had done. I had said the words I swore I would never say. It was almost as if the words hung visibly in the air. I could see them there, inside a cartoonist's word balloon. How could I have let those words slip out?

Of course, those are not the worst words I have ever said. Other words I have spoken have been hurtful or spiteful—not simply contrary to parenting advice. But this incident shows how difficult it is to control the tongue. Even words I promised myself I would never say tumbled out of my lips.

I was trying to wear Patient Peony, but I ended up putting Because-I-Said-So Bloom on my lips. If my most fervent resolutions and most determined efforts were not enough to restrain my lips, how could I ever change my speech? Was there any way to achieve a Mouth Makeover?

Top Ten Ways to Get Your Mouth in Trouble

1. Always talk. Never listen.

2. Interrupt when you have something to say.

3. Complain loudly about anything and everything.

4. Talk endlessly about yourself, your kids, your grandkids.

5. Be sure that everyone knows about your friend's embarrassing situation.

6. Speak before you think.

7. Make jokes about your spouse.

8. Let your mouth run on automatic when you're angry.

9. Nag! Nag! Nag!

10. Assume you can control your tongue on your own without God's help.

In the Old Testament, we are told about an extreme Mouth Makeover. This dramatic transformation happened to a man of God, a scribe who meticulously copied Scripture. No doubt he was a follower of God who conscientiously obeyed the Law. But the Lord gave him a vision that changed the way he looked at himself.

One day, this scribe was given a glimpse of heaven. In this peek into eternity, he saw the Lord seated on a high throne wearing a robe with a train so long it filled the temple. In breathless wonder, the scribe saw angels flying above God Almighty, singing majestic songs extolling His holiness and glory. The man of God was amazed that although these six-winged beings had never sinned against the Lord, they were so in awe of His glory that they used two of their wings to cover their faces. The scribe almost needed to cover his own ears as the glorious and overpowering sound of the angels' voices shook the doors of the temple.

In the sight of God's awesome holiness, the scribe was struck by his own unholiness. He realized his failures. He felt grimy, filthy. This scribe was so burdened by his transgressions that he wailed with a deep, guttural cry.

What had this man done that he was in such a state of despair? Had he struck someone? betrayed someone? killed someone?

The scribe in this story was the great prophet Isaiah. He was no doubt a faithful servant of God, but encountering the glory of God brought him face-to-face with his own sinfulness. The vision of a pure and holy God hit him with his own uncleanness. And he realized which part of him was dirty.

His mouth.

The prophet recorded his story in Isaiah 6. He told his readers that when he saw the Lord, all he could do was cry out, "Woe to me! For I am lost; for I am a man of unclean lips, and I dwell in the midst of a people of unclean lips; for my eyes have seen the King, the LORD of hosts!" (Isaiah 6:5). That first word, *woe*, is a passionate cry of grief or despair. Isaiah was utterly depressed about his condition. He realized he needed a Mouth Makeover.

What words had Isaiah spoken that caused him such distress? Had he cursed? lied? gossiped? Or like me, had he raised his voice at his children?

We don't know what specific words upset the prophet, but I think his anguish was caused by a new realization: His mouth had not only harmed people in his life, it had also wounded God.

Thinking about Isaiah's response, I realize that I often put my foot in my mouth and sometimes regret my words, but I may not be convicted about my lips. I may feel foolish and embarrassed, but do I lament the fact that I am actually hurting God with my mouth?

✝ *A true Mouth Makeover begins when I am not only embarrassed by my mouth mishaps but am aware that my hurtful words grieve God.*

Put yourself in the sandals of the scribe for a moment. If God gave you a 3-D surround sound experience of His holiness, what might your reaction be? What area of your life would make you feel uncomfortable? Would your mouth be the first thing you would cover up?

A Word of Forgiveness for Today

God begins our Mouth Makeover through Baptism by wiping off the stain of our guilt and cleansing our messy mouths.

Fortunately, when we look at ourselves in the mirror of God's Word and see that we've been wearing the shades of Insensitive Iris and Hurtful Hyacinth on our lips, we can begin a Mouth Makeover. When we are saddened by the color of our words, God begins the transformation. He does not leave us in a state of despair. Through the water and the Word of Holy Baptism, He begins the exfoliating process by wiping off the stain of our guilt and cleansing our messy mouths.

Heavenly Father, I know I have a messy mouth. Too often, I don't think before I speak and am embarrassed by what rolls off my tongue. But I realize now that my words also grieve You. I desire to change. Cleanse my messy mouth and help me start this day with pure words. In Jesus' name. Amen.

DAY 2

Lipstick Lesson

1. Have you worn any of these messy shades of speech? Check all that you have worn in the last week.

_____ Motormouth Mocha
_____ Nagging Nectarine
_____ Interrupting Ivory
_____ Boastful Burgundy
_____ Muttering Mulberry
_____ Angry Apricot
_____ Reckless Rose
_____ Hurtful Hyacinth
_____ Profane Peony
_____ Insensitive Iris
_____ Slander Scarlet
_____ Lying Lilac
_____ Belittling Berry
_____ Criticizing Cranberry
_____ Abusive Amethyst
_____ Whiny Watermelon
_____ Bossy Begonia
_____ Foot-in-Mouth Fuchsia

Why do you think you wore those messy shades? Stress? Fatigue? Habit? A difficult person? (If we examine the triggers to our regrettable words, we may be able to avoid them in the future.)

2. Read Isaiah 6:1–5. Answer the following questions:

   a. Why do you think the angels covered their faces and feet? How does seeing their response affect the way you approach God?

   b. The angels sang, "Holy, holy, holy is the LORD Almighty." The word *holy* has the idea of cleanness and purity, but also has a sense of apartness. God is set apart from creation—He is not created. He is totally unique. Will this truth affect your prayer life? How?

c. When the angels sang, the doorposts shook. Their words had power. Our words also have power. Name an instance where the words you spoke today had a positive effect:

d. What do you feel when you read Isaiah's reaction to seeing God's glory?

3. What key lesson did you learn today?

4. Our memory verse for this week is Psalm 19:14, "Let the words of my mouth and the meditation of my heart be acceptable in Your sight, O Lord, my rock and my redeemer." To help you memorize this verse, write the words here in your own handwriting.

Meaningful Makeover

God knows our shortcomings, but invites us to come to Him for forgiveness. Look again at the shades of messy speech you checked in Question 1 today. Write a prayer confessing those unattractive words and receive God's grace.

Laundered Lips

Behold, this has touched your lips; your guilt is taken away, and your sin atoned for. Isaiah 6:7

One hot, sultry summer day when I was a kid, my friends Nancy, Janet, and I were playing in their backyard, swinging, sliding, and working up a thirst. After a while we decided to go into the house to get a drink, but when Nancy poured out the lemonade, she spilled a little.

"Darn it," she said, running to the sink to get the dishcloth to mop up the spill.

Even though Nancy's mother was sitting in the living room, that naughty word reached her ears and soon her mom was dragging Nancy down the hall to the bathroom.

I asked Nancy's sister, Janet, what was happening.

"I'll bet she's going to get her mouth washed out with soap," Janet said.

Washed out with soap? I had never heard of this practice before and my child mind tried to figure out how that was going to help.

Then Nancy emerged out of the bathroom, a little lather still around her lips. She was wiping her mouth and spitting, trying to get rid of the dreadful taste. Then I got the idea. Nancy's mom was trying to clean Nancy's mouth and do it in a way that would leave a taste in her mouth that might make her think twice before she said "darn" again.

Remember the story of Isaiah? His taste of God's holiness made him painfully aware of the bad words he had said. But God did not use a bar of soap to clean out Isaiah's mouth. He used fire. One of the Lord's holy seraphs used tongs to grab a hot coal from God's altar. The angel touched the coal to Isaiah's mouth and said, "Behold, this has touched your lips; your guilt is taken away, and your sin atoned for" (Isaiah 6:7).

Isaiah recognized his messy mouth, but he could not fix it. Isaiah did not grab the purifying coal. God's angel did.

☩ *The trouble with talking too fast is you may say something you haven't thought of yet. Ann Landers*

We cannot buy magic makeup remover to fix our mouths. There is no special serum available that can wipe away the stain of Slander Scarlet or Reckless Rose. But God is able to cleanse our mouths. When we come with repentant hearts, He scrubs off the guilt. When we kneel at His Table, He removes the stain of our angry and hurtful words.

What a relief! My words have not measured up to the words God would like me to use. But once I have confessed my mouth mishaps, God offers the cleansing power of forgiveness.

Look at Isaiah's reaction to God's purifying process. Isn't it interesting to note that Isaiah does not scream in pain when the live coal touches his lips? He let out an agonizing yell of "Woe is me!" when faced with his own guilt, but the Bible does not record any cry of pain when the burning coal touched him. Perhaps this was because the relief of forgiveness was greater than any physical pain he felt.

Sometimes when I close my eyes at night, the events of the day replay in my mind. I remember a foolish remark I made. I recall words I spoke in impatience. Or I cringe, thinking of how I talked when I should have simply listened. I wonder, "Will I ever learn?"

It would be easy to feel hopeless about my mouth. To feel dejected about my inability to restrain my tongue. To wonder if I will ever be able to control my lips.

A Word of Forgiveness for Today
God uses the exfoliator of grace to scrub off the guilt of our words.

But when I discover I have once again used hurtful shades of speech, the grace of Jesus Christ that is ours through faith is the ultimate makeup remover. When I have neglected to wear the color of life-giving words, His mercy is available. I may still have to live with the consequences of my words, but I can go to the God of forgiveness and daily receive pardon. He will wipe away all the unattractive shades of speech and give me a new start. And thankfully, He won't use a bar of soap.

God of grace and mercy, sometimes I wonder if I will ever be able to control my mouth. I confess that I have spoken out of anger and impatience. I have complained and whined. Cleanse my mouth and scrub it with Your grace so that I can speak Your praise. In Jesus' name. Amen.

DAY 3

Lipstick Lesson

1. Have you ever witnessed someone getting their mouth washed out with soap? What was your reaction?

2. Read Isaiah 6:6–7. Put yourself in Isaiah's place. How would you feel after hearing the seraph's words?

3. What do the following verses say about forgiveness?

    a. Psalm 86:5:

    b. Colossians 1:13–14:

    c. 1 John 1:8–9:

    d. Have you acknowledged the gift of God's forgiveness or do you tend to continue to replay your mistakes in your mind? How can you grab onto the truth the angel spoke, "Your guilt is taken away, and your sin atoned for" (Isaiah 6:7)?

4. What key lesson did you learn today?

5. Write out this week's memory verse. Try not to peek!

Meaningful Makeover

As a way to visualize God's cleansing power of forgiveness, put on some lipstick and then watch yourself in the mirror as you wipe off its color. Thank God that He can remove the stain of messy speech from your lips. Here or in your journal, record your feelings about God's forgiveness.

DAY 4

Take Two

And I heard the voice of the Lord saying, "Whom shall I send,
and who will go for us?" Then I said, "Here I am! Send me."
Isaiah 6:8

I could feel my panic level rising. As I prepared for the making of a companion DVD for my book *Divine Design*, my anxiety grew. I was excited about the opportunity to be the speaker for a teaching video, but I was also scared to death! The usual comfort I felt talking in front of groups disappeared at the thought of speaking in front of cameras. Although I prepared as thoroughly as possible, the butterflies in my stomach fluttered wildly when the big day arrived. In fact, those butterflies were so active that I had to redo the beginning of the first segment four times.

By the time I got to the third segment, I began to relax a bit. Inside I was shouting a little "Woohoo!" when I got through the entire session in one take. After the closing prayer, I felt a sense of relief until—Peggy, my editor, approached me, "Sharla," she said, "that was a great dress rehearsal."

Dress rehearsal? What went wrong?

"We just noticed at the end of the session that you had lipstick on your teeth. Take two."

While I wasn't thrilled at the prospect of having to perform the third speech again, I was grateful for the chance for a do-over. Pink teeth are not a particularly glamorous look. The episode of lipstick-stained teeth ended up in some electronic trash bin and I was given a fresh start.

Tips for Keeping Lipstick Off Your Teeth

1. Apply petroleum jelly. Not on your lips, but on your teeth. A thin layer of petroleum jelly makes a slick coating that lipstick will have a hard time adhering to.

2. Set the color with a little loose powder. Separate a two-ply tissue into one-ply. Place the one-ply piece over your lips and dust on the powder. Just enough powder will go through the tissue to set the color.

3. Use your index finger. Poke your finger in your mouth, make an O with your mouth around your finger and pull your finger out. Any stray lipstick on your inner lip will stick to your finger.

I sure wish I had known these tips sooner! But I am thankful that God also gives me the opportunity for a new beginning. Even when my mouth is stained with speech in the shades of nagging, belittling, or grumbling, He forgives me and gives me opportunities to use my mouth in ways that please Him. God also gave Isaiah new opportunities for speaking once the prophet had realized the unclean state of his mouth and received the angel's purifying touch. After the angel told Isaiah, "Your guilt is taken away, and your sin atoned for" (Isaiah 6:7), God asked, "Whom shall I send, and who will go for us?" (Isaiah 6:8).

Are you surprised that God would offer Isaiah the opportunity to speak for Him? After all, the prophet had already come clean about his unclean lips. If he knew his mouth was dirty, certainly God was also aware of Isaiah's mouth problems. Yet God gives Isaiah the chance to be His spokesperson.

✝ *God's cleansing power gives us the opportunity to use our lips to serve Him.*

What was Isaiah's response? He had just been feeling totally despondent about the state of his mouth. Logic would tell me that the humble scribe would slink away, thinking the job of God's spokesman was way out of his reach. Let someone else more qualified take the position.

However, Isaiah shouts out, "Here I am! Send me" (Isaiah 6:8).

What made all of this possible? Forgiveness. Mercy. God's exfoliator of grace. God no longer saw any trace of unclean lips. He offered the cleansed Isaiah a new role, a chance to use his lips for the Lord.

Positive Ways to Use Our Lips

Once we have experienced God's grace, we are eager to use our lips to please God and bless others. Here are some positive ways to use our lips:

- Say thank you.
- Apologize.
- Talk about your faith.

25

- Give a sincere compliment.
- Recite Scripture.
- Quash gossip.
- Defend someone wrongly accused.
- Sing a song of praise.
- Relate a funny story.
- Pray.

And Isaiah? Because of God's action in his life, he went from "Woe is me" to "Here I am!" Depression to enthusiasm. Despondency to passion. He no longer felt the burden of his guilt, the stain of his unclean speech. His joy in forgiveness gave him the desire to serve the One who removed the uncleanness of his mouth and the weight of his sin.

> ✝ *My Mouth Makeover is a fashion statement*
> *of my internal spiritual makeover.*

God also offers us opportunities to serve Him with our lips. Once He has cleansed our lips from the effects of nagging, insensitivity, and criticizing, He gives us a whole new makeup bag stocked with encouragement, praise, and mercy. Thankfully, our mouth mishaps do not prevent us from participating in God's mission of sharing His grace. He extends His mercy to us, His baptized and forgiven daughters, and offers the chance to be a spokesperson for His love. Hear His words to you: "Take two!"

A Word of Forgiveness for Today

Once God has scrubbed my lips with His mercy, He no longer sees an unclean mouth.

Most Holy God, You know the state of my mouth. Still, You love me and "by the washing of regeneration and renewal of the Holy Spirit" (Titus 3:5), You offer the opportunity for a new start—a chance to speak for You. Continue to remind me that You have bestowed this gift of speech. Help me to use the gift well, embracing the mission to speak grace to others. In Jesus' name. Amen.

DAY 4

Lipstick Lesson

1. Have you ever wished for a do-over? Recall a time when your mouth messed up and you wished you could have a fresh start and summarize it here.

STEP 1

2. Read Isaiah 6:8. How did Isaiah respond to the forgiveness he received?

3. Are you willing to say, "Here I am! Send me"? Brainstorm and come up with three areas of your life where you could serve God with your mouth.

4. Read David's psalm of confession: Psalm 51.

   a. In the space following, write some of the phrases David uses to ask for forgiveness. What word pictures does he use? (vv. 1–12)

   b. Because of God's "steadfast love" (v. 1), David is confident of God's mercy. Write some phrases that describe our state after we've received forgiveness. (vv. 7–9)

   c. How will David use his mouth now that he is restored to God? (vv. 13–15)

5. What key lesson did you learn today?

6. Write out this week's memory verse. No peeking!

Meaningful Makeover

Choose a positive way to use your mouth today. Embrace your mission to be God's spokesperson to this dark world. Write here or in your journal how you shared words of grace, kindness, or love.

Telling Tongue

He said, "Go, and say to this people." Isaiah 6:9a

I have a friend who makes a point of speaking a word of blessing to every salesperson she encounters. As she takes her receipt or picks up her shopping bag from the counter, she looks the clerk in the eye and says, "God bless you. Have a great day."

Another friend of mine has the gift of encouragement. During fellowship time after church, Rhonda quietly seeks out people who are struggling with illness or grief. She listens attentively and offers a word of cheer.

My daughter, Anna, and her family have traveled halfway around the world to share the Good News of Jesus in China. They are studying the language and striving to use the new words they are learning in a way that will show the love of God.

These women are using their words to influence the world. They wear shades of speech that encourage and build up others. Like Isaiah, they embrace their mission to be God's spokesperson to a broken, hurting world.

After Isaiah volunteered, "Here I am! Send me." God immediately gave him an assignment. He said, "Go, and say to this people" (Isaiah 6:9). Our newly-cleansed mouths have a purpose. We are to speak life to the people in our lives.

Author Sharon Jaynes writes in her book *The Power of a Woman's Words*:

> God has given us incredible power in our sphere of influence,
> and it begins with the words we speak. Few forces have
> as powerful an effect as the sounds that pass our lips. Our
> words can spark a child to accomplish great feats, encourage
> a husband to conquer the world, fan the dying embers of a
> friend's broken dreams into flame, encourage a fellow believer
> to run the race set before her, and draw a lost soul to Christ.[2]

Picture the words you speak as treasured gifts to the people around you. Hold out the present of hope, the gift of encouragement, the offering of comfort.

If you continued reading in Isaiah 6, you would see that the message Isaiah was to share was one of judgment. Sometimes we are called on to share difficult words, but more often the words that God tells us to give others are words that build up His people in Christ. Later on in the Book of Isaiah, the prophet wrote, "The Lord GOD has given me the tongue of those who are taught, that I may know how to sustain with a word him who is weary. Morning by morning He awakens; He awakens my ear to hear as those who are taught" (Isaiah 50:4).

Isaiah spoke words that encouraged those who were tired and gave strength to those who were ready to give up. I hope I can do the same. I want my words to support my friends when they're struggling, to strengthen my husband when he's tired, to build up my children when they are discouraged.

Five Practical Suggestions to Assist You in Your Mouth Makeover

1. Be aware of the people you hang out with. Some people seem to be chronic gossips or constant complainers. You may need to limit your time with them or be ready to steer the conversation into more positive waters.

2. Count to ten. It's an old technique, but an effective one when you're upset or angry.

3. Try to see things from a different perspective. When you're in a difficult conversation, ask God to help you to see things from the other person's point of view.

4. Know your triggers. When is your mouth most likely to misbehave? In the car? With a difficult person in your life? Be prepared to be extra diligent and prayerful in those situations.

5. Get enough sleep! I've found that my mouth is much more likely to do damage when the rest of my body is tired. Obtaining the rest we need whenever possible may be one of the best antidotes to mouth mayhem.

But where do I get these words? Speaking whatever first pops into my mind does not usually get the results I want. Like Isaiah, I have to listen to God. I need to learn from the God who spoke the world into being. I need instruction from Jesus, who spoke mercy to the men pounding nails into His hands. I need to listen to the Holy Spirit, who gave the disciples life-changing words for those who did not know the Savior. In other words, I need the Word.

A Word of Forgiveness for Today

The Lord speaks words of forgiveness to me when I have failed. He whispers words of hope to me when I am weary, that I might speak the same for others.

Use Isaiah's experience to shape your words. Confess your unclean lips, and receive God's forgiveness. Offer your lips as a tool for God's use. Ask God to instruct your tongue and speak words that encourage those who are tired and weary.

You may not care about lip exfoliators. Fancy lip products may not appeal to you. Perhaps you do not wear lipstick. That's okay. But let's plan to wear shades of speech that are life-giving. Let's look for words that color our world with hope. Let's approach each day as an opportunity to speak God's words.

Think of how you can use your lips to positively transform your sphere of influence. Listen to God's words of comfort and grace to you and share them with the people in your life. Bless a store clerk. Encourage a friend whose shoulders are sagging. Share Christ's love with those who do not yet know Him.

Precious Jesus, I am anxious to begin a Mouth Makeover. I confess I have spoken insensitive and unkind words. Cleanse my mouth and make it fit for You. Thank You for Your exfoliator of grace and the opportunity to share Your love. Give me words to sustain the weary and tired people I see all around me. Here I am, send me! Amen.

DAY 5

Lipstick Lesson

1. Which of the five practical suggestions for a Mouth Makeover will you use this week? Record your plan to implement it here:

2. LIP Study. Each week, we will closely examine one section of Scripture using a three-step process. This study style has made me a better student of the Bible. It has helped me to notice things in God's Word that I have previously missed, to pay attention to the details, and, most important, to hear God speak. You will read the passage three times each time looking for something new following the acronym LIP:

Look for the Facts

Interpret the Meaning

Pursue the Application

James, the brother of Jesus, had a lot to say about taming the tongue. Read James 3:1–10 and use the following study guide (I have done a few verses for you as examples):

Look for the facts. Don't make any interpretations here. Simply write what is happening in each verse.

Verse 1 Not many should become teachers.

Verse 2 We all stumble in many ways. A person who has no fault in what he says is perfect.

Verse 3 A small bit in a horse's mouth controls this large animal.

Verse 4 Large ships can be driven by a small rudder.

Verse 5 The tongue is capable of great boasts. A large fire can be started by a small spark.

Verse 6

Verse 7

Verse 8

Verse 9

Verse 10

Interpret the meaning. Turn the lesson in the passage into a scriptural principle. Example:

Verse 1 Teachers will be judged more strictly.

Verse 2 It is very difficult to control our words.

Verse 3 With the grace of God, we can bridle the tongue and change its course from harm to help.

Verse 4 Though the tongue is small, it can cause a great deal of good or a great deal of harm.

Verse 5 A small slip of the tongue can cause big problems.

Verse 6

Verse 7

Verse 8

Verse 9

Verse 10

Pursue the application. Turn the principle you discovered into a personal question that applies the truth to your life. Example:

Verse 1 If I want to be a teacher, am I willing to be held to a higher standard? Do I judge teachers more strictly?

Verse 2 Since it is so difficult to control my words, am I remembering to ask God for help?

Verse 3 How can I better bridle my tongue?

Verse 4 Do I recognize the effect my words have on the people in my life?

Verse 5 When have I experienced the negative effects of the tongue?

Verse 6

Verse 7

Verse 8

Verse 9

Verse 10

3. What key lesson did you learn today?

4. Write out Psalm 19:14 from memory.

Meaningful Makeover

Choose one question from those you posed in "Pursue the Application." Answer it honestly and come up with an action you can do to grow in that area. For instance, in verse 2, I asked, "Since it is so difficult to control my words, am I remembering to ask God for help?" One way I can remind myself to remember to pray for God's help with my words is to write out the prayer on page 31 and post the prayer on my mirror and computer.

Soothe: Comfort with Encouragement

Memory Verse

Let no corrupting talk come out of your mouths, but only such as is good for building up, as fits the occasion, that it may give grace to those who hear. Ephesians 4:29

Slander Scarlet

Let no corrupting talk come out of your mouths, but only such
as is good for building up, as fits the occasion, that it may
give grace to those who hear. Ephesians 4:29

"You should have seen how my husband dressed the kids for church. They looked more like they were ready for a costume party than Sunday School!"

"Oh that's nothing. Mine surprised me by making dinner—using every pot and pan we own. I did dishes for two hours after I put the kids to bed."

"At least he tried to be helpful. My husband comes home and takes a nap—complaining what a hard day he's had. Let him chase two toddlers around all day—then he'd really know what a tough day was like!"

You may recognize this conversation. It's part of a game played regularly by some wives called Pin-the-Tale-on-the-Hubby. As a young mom, I remember sitting around with other mothers at play groups, swimming lessons, and baseball games when a round of this husband-bashing game would start up. Soon I found myself joining in, telling some funny story about my husband that did not paint him in the best light, but drew a laugh. We all bonded over how clueless our husbands could be about raising kids, housekeeping, or women in general. We felt better for venting our frustrations, convinced that men were hopeless.

Sometimes I would feel a little guilty after playing the game. Those words left a funny taste in my mouth. It also left an unattractive stain on my lips. I was wearing the shade of Slander Scarlet, but I didn't see it. I rationalized that I hadn't said anything terrible. I had simply told a story that other women could relate to. What did it hurt? We were merely voicing our complaints.

But, of course, our conversations did hurt. Perhaps our husbands never heard our complaints, but we were tearing them down. Ephesians 4:29 says, "Let no corrupting talk come out of your mouths, but only such as is good for building up." In the Greek, the word for corrupting means rotten and putrid. Our words about our husbands would have made them feel rotten. And we certainly were not building them up. Our little husband-bashing game may have let off a little steam, making my friends and me feel a little better, but it damaged our marriages.

✝ *God forbids us to slander our neighbor or hurt our neighbor's reputation.*
(Luther's Small Catechism)

That funny taste I had in my mouth didn't stop me from playing the game for very long. But one night during a Bible study meeting, my friend, Mary, talked about her mother who had passed away a few years earlier. Mary told us that at the funeral one of her mother's friends told her, "Your mother was such a wonderful person. She never said a bad word about anyone."

Suddenly, I felt the unattractive stain on my lips. I was sure that no one would say that about me. Not that I spread gossip, leaked secrets, or purposely lied about someone, but surely hurtful words, complaining words, negative words about other people had slipped out of my mouth, as evidenced in my participation in Pin-the-Tale-on-the-Hubby.

Mary's comment about her mother was in response to our study about slander. First Peter 2:1 says, "So put away all malice and all deceit and hypocrisy and envy and all slander." I always thought I was pretty safe with the slander thing. After all, slander in our country is defined as telling lies about someone to hurt their reputation. I may have said hurtful things, but at least they were true!

A Word of Encouragement for Today

God's grace through Christ Jesus forgives when my words have wounded spirits and torn hearts.

I felt smug in my innocence until I looked up slander in my Greek dictionary. I found out the word for slander in Greek is *katalalia*, formed from two root words: *kata* meaning "against" and *laleo* meaning "to speak." This informed me that slander in the New Testament meant any evil speaking against someone—true or false. Katalalia is also translated as back-biting, hurtful talk, or unkind speech. I no longer felt so self-righteous. A lot of those "mom-therapy sessions" included hurtful talk and unkind speech. I don't think we set out to wound our husbands, but certainly we did not build them up. We were, in fact, using the shade of Slander Scarlet when we got together.

> If God were hosting a *What Not to Say* television show, here are some examples He might give us in "What Not to Say" and "What to Say" to our husbands.

What Not to Say	What to Say
"You're wearing *that*?"	"I really like you in the blue shirt. Maybe you could wear that today."
"You'll never amount to anything."	"Don't give up. I believe in you."
"I told you so."	"Things didn't work out this time. But I know you did your best."
"I don't know what I was thinking when I married you!"	"I'm frustrated now. How can we work this out?"
"Oh good, you're home. Can you take out the garbage?"	"It's so nice to have you home."

I determined to change my ways. When my friends started up another round of the husband-bashing game, I kept quiet. Even when I had a story I knew would amuse everyone, I bit my tongue. Then I decided to take it a step further and end the game abruptly by changing the subject. And sometimes, I even started a new game by saying something positive about my husband. This brought the conversation to a grinding halt for a minute or two, but usually someone joined the new game and also praised her spouse. Soon everyone found something good to say, and when our husbands came home, we were more likely to greet them with appreciation instead of disgruntled complaints.

✝ *Slander Scarlet is the shade of speech that leaves a stain on another person's character. It is the color we wear whenever we engage in back-biting talk, hurtful words, or belittling speech.*

Dear friends, it's time we stop wearing the lip color called Slander Scarlet. The next step in our makeover is to realize that with our mouths we have the capability to do much damage, but we also can soothe and heal. Instead of tearing people down with our lips, let's build them up. Although Back-biting Bronze and Hurtful Hyacinth are popular lip stains, choose instead Positive Pink.

Heavenly Father, forgive me when I have used my lips to tear people down. Pardon my insulting and back-biting comments. Help me use my mouth to say positive words and not negative ones about the people in my life. In Jesus' name. Amen.

DAY 1

Lipstick Lesson

1. This week, we are focusing on getting rid of hurtful, back-biting words and replacing them with positive, soothing speech. Lip balm soothes our own lips. Do you use a lip balm? Tell about your favorite product.

2. Have you ever participated in the "husband-bashing game"? Or have you witnessed the sport of "friend-knocking"? Why do you think we sometimes like to play these games?

3. Today's lesson is about the lip stain of Slander Scarlet. Following are a few synonyms of *slander*. Look them up in a dictionary and write short definitions here.

   a. insult

   b. malign

   c. slur

   d. disparage

   e. smear

   Using what you just discovered, how would you define slander?

4. What do these verses say about slander?

   a. Psalm 15:1–3

   b. Psalm 101:5

   c. James 4:11–12

5. What key lesson did you learn today?

6. Write out our memory verse for this week: "Let no corrupting talk come out of your mouths, but only such as is good for building up, as fits the occasion, that it may give grace to those who hear" (Ephesians 4:29). To help you memorize this passage, write it in the space below. You might also put on some lip balm and practice saying this verse in front of a mirror.

Meaningful Makeover

Today pay attention to what you say about other people. Are you wearing Slander Scarlet and using unkind, hurtful words? Or do you build others up? Use your journal or the space below to write what you discovered about your words.

Wounding Words

How long will you torment me and break me in pieces with words? Job 19:2

As an earnest young man sat diligently working on his art project, the school principal strolled through the room and inspected the work of the eighth graders. He noticed this industrious young student's work and picked up his drawing.

"Look at this!" the principal announced as he held up the picture before the whole class. The boy's heart filled with hope like a balloon with helium—the principal liked his artwork! The principal continued, "John doesn't have an ounce of artistic talent, but he's really trying."

The balloon popped.

The student in the story is my husband. He has repeatedly proven that principal wrong with his many outstanding woodworking projects. It turned out that his talent was in wood and not drawing. But that didn't make the principal's words sting any less when John was thirteen.

Our words can fill a heart with hope, joy, and confidence. But they can also deflate a heart just as easily. What we say can shatter a spirit, crush a dream, or fracture a hope. What leaves our lips can puncture a tender soul, sever a delicate relationship, or tear a fragile faith. Our mouths can be dangerous weapons, tearing down, rather than building up. The next step in our Mouth Makeover is to eliminate negative speech and instead use the soothing balm of encouragement.

Recipe for Homemade Lip Balm

Encouragement is like balm to a hurting soul. Try making this homemade lip balm—when you smooth it on your lips, let it remind you to spread some encouragement around as well.

- 3 tsp. grated beeswax or beeswax pellets
- 5 tsp. carrier oil (sunflower, coconut, calendula, even olive)
- 5–7 drops of essential oil (lime, lemon, peppermint, etc.)
- ½ tsp. honey (for flavor, optional)

1. Put some water (about 1½ c.) in a pot on the stove and heat to boiling. Place the beeswax and carrier oil in a glass measuring cup and put the measuring cup in the boiling water. Stir as the two ingredients melt and mix.

2. Once they are completely melted, remove the measuring cup from the boiling water (use oven mitts) and set it on a heat-safe surface. Stir in the essential oil and honey if you are using it. Stir well.

3. Pour into containers. You can buy small jars specifically made for lip balm or reuse old jars you already have. The lip balm is ready to use when it solidifies.

What shade of lipstick are you wearing? Are the words leaving your mouth in the colors of discouragement, criticism, and debasement? Let's avoid the tainted shades of Pessimistic Plum, Criticizing Cranberry, and Belittling Berry.

PESSIMISTIC PLUM

What are you more likely to do? Fan to life a flickering dream or throw a bucketful of water to extinguish it forever? Author Deborah Smith Pegues writes, "An untold number of individuals have missed their destiny because of someone's discouraging words."[3]

At times, it is necessary to point out the pitfalls of a plan or warn against a goal that is not God-pleasing. However, whenever we can, let's cheer on our families and friends to pursue the calling God has placed in their hearts. Walk with them in hope, support, and prayer as they follow His path.

CRITICIZING CRANBERRY

Sharon Jaynes, in her book *The Power of a Woman's Words*, shares these findings, "Studies show that in the average home, ten negative comments are made for every positive one."[4] How would you describe the atmosphere in your home? Are you more likely to criticize than praise? Somehow it often seems easier to voice a complaint than to take the time to extend a word of appreciation.

However, our families, friends, and co-workers desperately need that positive word. Jaynes also says that "it takes four positive comments to counteract one negative comment."[5] When spirits are cut with criticism, it takes many positive words to heal the wound. Let's try to be the healers instead of the hurters.

A Word of Encouragement for Today

God's words to you: You are loved, you are valuable. You are accepted because of Jesus' sacrifice.

BELITTLING BERRY

I once knew a hilarious married couple. They constantly kept me in stitches. There was only one problem. The jokes were often told at the other spouse's expense. The remarks were witty and amusing, but always had a cutting edge. After awhile I didn't find them so funny. I imagined what the wife felt like when her husband delivered a barb. I sensed the pain in the husband's heart when his wife's joke cut deep. I wondered how long that marriage would last.

Our words can slice like a knife, causing pain, cutting tender souls. So I need to examine my words. Do they make the other person feel incapable or inadequate? Do I crush her spirit until she feels worthless or unimportant?

Instead, I want my mouth to express worth and acceptance. I hope my lips make other people feel loved and appreciated. I will try to communicate how precious and priceless my loved ones are to me.

Let's throw out any lip product in the shades of Pessimistic Plum, Criticizing Cranberry, or Belittling Berry. Instead of breaking hearts with words, let's learn how to communicate words of praise, admiration, and worth.

Encouragement Blitz

An Encouragement Blitz is a simple, fun way to encourage in a group setting. This is a good activity to play as a family during a long car trip, at dinnertime, or during a family meeting. It could also be used by adult groups like your Bible study bunch or a committee that you are working on.

Each person gets to be the focus of an encouragement blitz. During that person's turn, his or her role is simply to listen without saying anything.

For sixty seconds, everyone else calls out all the things that they love, admire, or respect about the focus person.

It is helpful to use "I" phrases. For instance: "I love your smile." "I admire your perseverance." "I appreciate your help with the dishes."[6]

Lord Jesus, I know that I sometimes use critical and discouraging words. Help me to be aware of the cutting effect my speech can have. Teach my mouth to express words of acceptance and appreciation. In Your name. Amen.

DAY 2

Lipstick Lesson

1. What is your reaction to the statistic that in the average American home ten negative comments are made for every positive one?

2. Give some examples of words spoken by people who were wearing the following shades of speech:

    a. Pessimistic Plum

    b. Criticizing Cranberry

    c. Belittling Berry

    Talk about how you have felt when you have received words in these colors.

3. The Book of Numbers in the Old Testament tells about men who spoke discouraging and pessimistic words. Read Numbers 13–14.

    a. What was the role of the men who gave a discouraging report? (13:17–20)

    b. How did they discourage the Israelites? (13:28–29, 31–33)

    c. What was the result? (14:1–4, 26–35)

    d. What happened to the discouragers? (14:36–37)

    e. Who were the lone encouragers and how were they able to give positive rather than negative words? (14:6–9)

f. What can you learn from this story that will help you become an encourager rather than a discourager?

4. What key lesson did you learn today?

5. Write out our memory verse for this week: "Let no corrupting talk come out of your mouths, but only such as is good for building up, as fits the occasion, that it may give grace to those who hear" (Ephesians 4:29). Read a phrase, then cover it and write it. Recite as much of the verse as you can without looking.

Meaningful Makeover

Today evaluate your speech in terms of the positive and negative quality of your words. Are you communicating discouraging, critical, and belittling words? Or are you offering words of encouragement, praise, and worth? Use the space below to journal about your words.

DAY 3

Conveying Confidence

STEP 2:

And Jesus answered him, "Blessed are you, Simon Bar-Jonah! For flesh and blood has not revealed this to you, but My Father who is in heaven." Matthew 16:17

How did Jesus build up the people in His life? Imagine what it would be like to physically be with Christ every day. Picture yourself walking along the road with the most loving person you could ever know. Imagine sitting at the Great Teacher's feet. Envision witnessing the power of the Great Healer.

As one of the Twelve, you might wonder why Jesus chose you. You're not the best educated. Sometimes you are a little impetuous. You've been known to put your foot in your mouth.

Yet Jesus loves *you!* You can see the love in His eyes. Once in a while, however, you also see disappointment. At times, He has said to you, "I can't believe how small your faith is!" You are stricken with remorse when you see the hurt in His eyes. More than anything else, you want to please this Man, your God, the Messiah. Yet, too often your actions seem to have the opposite effect.

Just the other day, Jesus was telling your group to be careful of the teachings of the Pharisees, a self-righteous sect of the Jews. He had talked about yeast to illustrate their influence, and none of you understood. Everyone thought He was criticizing the group for not bringing bread along, and again you heard those words, "O you of little faith." You could hear a little frustration in His voice.

But today was different. Instead of putting your foot in your mouth again, you said something right! While you were walking with the other disciples and the Teacher, He asked, "What are the people saying about Me?" Some in the group chimed in, "Some say you're John the Baptist, some think you are Elijah, others think you must be Jeremiah or another prophet."

Then Jesus asked, "Who do you say that I am?" And you replied (the first to speak, as usual), "You are the Messiah, the Son of the living God." Jesus turned toward you, put His hands on your shoulders, looked you in the eyes and said,

"Blessed are you! The words you have spoken have been given to you by the Father in heaven. These words of faith will be the foundation of the Church."

Jesus turned and started walking again, but your feet were rooted to the ground. You almost could not believe what had just happened. You opened your mouth and what came out was right! Jesus was pleased. The Savior expressed confidence—in you!

Perhaps you remember this story recorded in Matthew 16:5–19 and recognize the main protagonist as the disciple Peter. Perhaps you can relate to this ever-impulsive apostle. His mouth always seemed to be getting him in trouble. He always seemed to say the wrong thing. Perhaps he felt useless and hopeless. At times, he probably wondered if he should just go back to fishing.

He may have asked himself, "How could God use my mouth?"

I often feel like this. How could God use my lips? When I forget to consider other's feelings, one look at those lips reveals the shade of Belittling Berry. When I neglect to encourage my family and friends, you can tell I've been using a tube of Criticizing Cranberry. When I speak before thinking, I find myself wearing Foot-in-Mouth Fuchsia. Again.

But I take comfort in the fact that Christ did not give up on Peter. Jesus didn't send His impetuous disciple home the first time his mouth got ahead of his brain. Our Savior didn't expel him from disciple school when he spoke without thinking. Christ didn't say, "Peter, I don't think I can use you."

When I've made yet another mouth mistake, I sometimes wonder if Jesus is exasperated with me. But when I observe how Jesus treated Peter, I remember my Savior's patience. He doesn't throw up His arms in resignation when I've spoken unkind words about my friend. He doesn't roll His eyes and cross His arms in frustration when I could have spoken an encouraging word, but was too busy thinking about myself.

A Word of Encouragement for Today

The Lord will not expel you from disciple school when you have experienced failure. He has a plan to graduate you to a new level of service.

Jesus holds out His arms in forgiveness. He gives me the strength to do better next time.

Jesus told Peter that his words of faith were given to him by the Father. God will also give us words of faith, words of hope, words of encouragement. On our own, our tongues will get tangled in negative words, but the Holy Spirit can help us to wear the positive shade of Cheering Cherry. I pray that instead of making people feel worthless and inadequate, my words will express their importance and value. I hope that my words will mend hearts and restore relationships instead of damage souls and injure spirits. I pray that my mouth will become skilled in the art of encouragement.

Encouraging Words for the People in Your Life

- Voice confidence in their abilities—assure them they can do it.

- Use specific praise—tell them exactly what you appreciate about them or their work.

- Try indirect praise—commend their efforts in front of others.

- Express genuine interest in their pursuits—ask questions about something important to them.

- Take notice of their efforts—comment on any improvement you see.

- Compliment sincerely—especially when they're not expecting it.

Holy Spirit, You are the Great Encourager and Comforter. Help me to remember that You have also given me the power to comfort and strengthen the people I care about. Give me renewing words, affirming words, and cheering words to share with the broken people in my life. Amen.

DAY 3

Lipstick Lesson

1. What is your reaction to the story of Peter told in today's lesson?

2. Now read the story in Matthew 16:5–20.

   a. Speculate how Peter might have felt after Jesus' words in verses 8–11.

   b. Now imagine Peter's emotions after Jesus' words in verses 17–19.

   c. Jesus calls Peter blessed. In the Greek, this word is *makarios,* which can mean happy or possessing the favor of God. How do these two meanings apply to Peter here?

   d. Examine Jesus' words in verses 17–19. What are some elements of Jesus' encouraging speech?

   e. How can you use these elements in your words today?

3. What key lesson did you learn today?

4. Write out this week's memory verse. Try not to peek.

Meaningful Makeover

Imagine yourself as Peter in today's Matthew reading. Write a prayer expressing your thoughts to Jesus as if He were standing next to you. Are you feeling discouraged? thankful? repentant? End the prayer by asking Christ for words of encouragement to pass on to others today. Later, examine the day: how did that prayer affect your words?

DAY 4

The Buildup

Therefore encourage one another and build one another up, just as you are doing. 1 Thessalonians 5:11

My son, Nathaniel, has the gift of encouragement. In fact, he has possessed this gift from a very young age. Sometimes this talent has surprised even me.

When Nathaniel was four, he was in Mrs. Holmes's Sunday School class. She is a marvelous, creative teacher and gifted in the art of encouraging her students. One day, after all the Sunday School classes were dismissed and children came flying down the hall waving pictures of Jesus and brand-new craft projects, Mrs. Holmes joined the madhouse of parents and kids in the vestibule. She approached me and said, "You'll never guess what Nathaniel said in Sunday School today." My mind raced, quickly reviewing the past week, trying to remember any potentially embarrassing incident that a four-year-old might have chosen to relate.

Mrs. Holmes saw the look of horror on my face and quickly continued, "No, no, don't worry! After the lesson, I told the class, 'Thank you for being such good students today!' and Nathaniel said, 'Thank you for being such a good teacher today!'"

I was amazed. And proud! My four-year-old son had complimented his teacher and made her day.

If a four-year-old can learn to encourage others, maybe I can too.

Yesterday we read a story about the impulsive apostle Peter. Although I can relate to him and his mouth mishaps, it is Jesus I want to emulate. Our Savior's words give us an example of building up others. No one looking at Peter in his early years would have guessed that his words would lead thousands to life-changing faith. But Jesus could see beyond Peter's limitations. The very first time the two met, Jesus told this disciple he would no longer be called Simon but would instead be called Peter, which means "rock." Certainly Simon Peter more often acted impetuously, not steadfastly like a rock, but Jesus encouraged Peter with this new name. He expressed confidence that His friend would develop an immovable faith. And He sent His Holy Spirit to give Peter the right words.

Just as Jesus encouraged Peter, it is my job to build up the people in my life. The apostle Paul tells us, "Therefore encourage one another and build one another up, just as you are doing" (1 Thessalonians 5:11). It is not difficult to find people who need encouragement. They are in the aisles of the grocery store, in the cubicles of our workplace, in the pews in our church. They are even in the chairs at our own kitchen table.

✞ *Make it a part of your "makeup routine" to wear Cheering Cherry every day. Look for opportunities to encourage and build up the people who pass through your life.*

Cultivate the habit of noticing people who pass through your life who may need a refreshing word or appreciative comment. Observe the tired cashier in the grocery store. Perceive your husband's disappointment. Calvin Miller, the author of *The Power of Encouragement*, wrote, "We must go into all the world and redeem it from the paralysis of hurt. We must find those who are shattered and love them back together again. We have freely received grace, and we must freely distribute grace as well."[7]

How can we distribute grace? Some people, like my son, are natural encouragers. But even if we do not have the gift of encouragement, God asks us to build each other up. And we can learn how from the support we ourselves have received.

A Word of Encouragement for Today
Jesus lavishly dispenses grace, redeeming lives and healing hearts.

I'm grateful for verbal encouragement. Positive comments about my hair or clothes can make my day. Applause for my efforts can make my week. Being asked if I'm my daughter's sister can make my year!

✞ *I can live for two months on a good compliment. Mark Twain*

I appreciate written encouragement too. In fact, I save cherished cards and letters in a special box. When I'm feeling blue, I drag the box out of my closet and read some of the affirmations I have received over the years.

Encouraging Actions for the People in Your Life

- Use the phone—let someone know you're thinking of them.

- Send an e-mail—a quick way to offer support.

- Tuck in a note—in a lunchbox or briefcase or on a pillow.

- Send a card—getting a beautiful card in the mailbox is a treat in this digital age.

- Give a gift—big or small, it can make someone feel special.

I treasure gifts of encouragement. The first time my daughter and her husband and baby went to China to serve for nine months, my heart ached in their absence. My friend, Sophie, helped ease the loneliness by sending me flowers on the day after they left. The card read, "Thinking of you. Nine months will go fast." Then when the unthinkable happened and Sophie was killed in a car accident, my friend, Gail, gave me an angel figurine to remind me of this special sister in Christ. Both gifts gave me comfort. The thoughtfulness of these friends reminded me of Christ's care.

With the help of the Holy Spirit, I am attempting to learn from these examples and step out of my usual self-centeredness. It takes a little work—encouragement isn't always my first response. But I am beginning to notice hurting people in my life and to take the time to build them up.

Wouldn't our homes be more like sanctuaries if encouragement were offered in daily doses? Wouldn't our workplaces be more like retreats if affirmations were regularly measured out? Wouldn't the world be a better place if every time we faced a disappointment, experienced a loss, or had a devastating failure, someone provided us with a small shot of Christ's mercy? Let's pray that God will open our eyes to see the hidden aches in peoples' souls and give us the words to support their faith and heal their hurts.

Dear Father in heaven, You see hurting souls in this world. Give me the eyes to see them too. Help me to take my focus off my own heartaches and to find meaningful ways to share Your comfort and grace with those who need Your healing touch. In Jesus' name. Amen.

DAY 4

Lipstick Lesson

1. Below are some phrases of praise. Add a few of your own. Share them in your group and make a point to use one to encourage someone today!

    "You've outdone yourself!"

    "I'm proud of you."

    "I am so grateful for you."

    "You have had a profound effect on my life."

    _____

    _____

    _____

2. What do the following verses say about encouraging and building others up?

    a. Romans 14:19

    b. Romans 15:2

    c. 1 Thessalonians 5:14

3. Here are some synonyms of *encourage:* cheer, refresh, inspire, affirm, praise. Look up each word in a dictionary, and using what you have learned from these synonyms and the Bible verses, write your own definition of *encourage.*

4. What key lesson did you learn today?

5. Write out this week's memory verse. No peeking!

Meaningful Makeover

In your journal, or in the space below, write the names of the key people in your life. Beside each name, write a couple of ways that you could specifically encourage them. Perhaps you will want to use some of the ideas from the lists of "Encouraging Words for the People in Your Life" (p. 48) and "Encouraging Actions for the People in Your Life" (p. 52). Choose one of those actions to do today. Pray that God will help you to become an encourager and daily support others.

KEY PEOPLE IN MY LIFE   **SPECIFIC WAYS TO ENCOURAGE**

The Power of Encouragement

See to it, brothers, that none of you has a sinful, unbelieving heart that turns away from the living God. But encourage one another daily, as long as it is called Today, so that none of you may be hardened by sin's deceitfulness. Hebrews 3:12–13 NIV

When our first grandson was seventeen months old, my husband and I traveled to Texas to visit him (and his parents). We could hardly wait to hug them and see their smiles in person. But we were a little concerned about our grandson's reaction. After not seeing us for three months, would Aaron remember us? Would he let us hold him? Or would he shy away from us?

On the day of our arrival, we landed at the Dallas airport in the early evening and decided to stop at a Denny's restaurant for supper. We sat at an empty table and ordered cheeseburgers and shakes. While we were waiting for our order, my daughter asked Aaron, "Are you glad Grandma and Grandpa came to visit?" Without hesitation, Aaron shouted, "Amen!"

Most of the restaurant heard that loud affirmation and we laughed out loud. But that one word made a world of difference to us. Our grandson was glad to see us. We were going to have a great time!

Isn't it amazing what an encouraging word can do?

Five Ways to Encourage Your Children

1. Catch them doing something right and comment on it! Too often, we only mention their negative behavior.

2. Express appreciation when your children are cooperative and helpful. Don't take their efforts for granted.

3. Praise and encourage a child for his efforts and not natural talent. Research shows that praising natural intelligence or talent may make children overly conscious of their image or become perfectionists.

4. Praise improvement and progress. Nobody is perfect and we shouldn't expect perfection from our children.

5. Have some fun together. Simply doing something fun with your kids will show them that you enjoy their company.

According to the Bible, we are to share encouraging words often. The Book of Hebrews tells us to "encourage one another daily" (Hebrews 3:13 NIV). A regular dose of verbal support can fuel our faith in God and assist our personal growth. Calvin Miller wrote, "All of us possess a wonderful power to touch other's lives. It is the power of affirmation! Why don't we use it? The world is waiting to be renewed, and we hold the power of renovation."[8]

Remember how Jesus gave Simon the solid new name of Peter (meaning "rock")? I'm sure this new moniker inspired Peter to venture out in trust. Jesus' expression of confidence gave His apostle the strength to persevere in his faith walk. Over the years, Peter attempted to act out the rocklike trust Christ saw in him, yet he often failed.

A Word of Encouragement for Today

On my own, my faith wobbles and falters. The Holy Spirit strengthens my weak knees and supports me when I stumble.

Then one day, Peter spoke up in his usual impulsive way, but with a different result. Peter spoke out of that unshakable faith and expressed his confidence in Jesus the Messiah, the Son of the living God. Jesus affirmed His confidence in His disciple. Jesus told Peter that his confession of the Christ would be the foundation of the Church. He informed Peter that he was blessed—that the heavenly Father Himself had revealed the truth to him.

Do you think Jesus' words of affirmation made a difference in Peter's life? It is difficult to imagine those comments not instilling in Peter a new confidence and sense of purpose. Certainly, he did not suddenly become perfect. He was still the disciple who impulsively but foolishly asked if they should erect some tents for Jesus, Moses, and Elijah at the transfiguration. He was still the disciple who denied Christ on the eve of His crucifixion. But later, on Pentecost, he was also the disciple who gave a sermon to thousands. Under the influence of the Holy Spirit, Peter was starting to live out Jesus' vision; he was becoming a firm example of faith.

I pray that my words will also speak confidence into those who are dear to me. I know I have experienced that type of support at times in my life. When I was growing up, my third-grade teacher, Faye Marquardt, became a friend of my family and a lifelong influence to me. She was a music lover and continually encouraged me in my piano and organ studies. Although I was a very average student, she made me feel like I had potential. Faye patiently listened to halting performances of hymns. She purchased organ books for me and encouraged me to play in an organ festival. I believe her confidence in me enabled me to complete a music degree.

✞ *Recklessly dispense encouragement to people you meet each day. Generously issue words of affirmation to friends you care about. Lavishly spread grace to those you love.*

Our words can be the wet blanket that stifles the flames of dreams or the little puff of air that will keep the embers glowing. I pray that I will be like Faye and offer words that give others the courage to pursue a new goal. I hope to be like Jesus, who looked past imperfections and saw potential, who pardoned stumbling, faltering attempts and envisioned rock-solid faith, who lavishly dispensed His grace to us "while we were still sinners" (Romans 5:8).

The simple tool of encouragement can cheer someone, fuel her determination, and strengthen her faith. We all have access to this potent lip product, yet we tend to ignore it in our makeup bag. Let's all toss out all the tubes of Belittling Berry and Slander Scarlet. Instead, let's receive comfort from the Great Encourager and pass it on to others with words in shades of inspiration and support.

> *Savior, I want my words to please You. Help me to speak words of confidence to the faltering and words of support to the weak. Help me to see others as You do, looking past their shortcomings and seeing their potential. Help me give voice to Your love. In Your name. Amen.*

DAY 5

Lipstick Lesson

1. When have you experienced the power of encouragement? Talk about someone who positively influenced your life through encouragement.

STEP 2

2. LIP Study. This week, we will study Luke 1:39–45 and discover how Elizabeth encouraged Mary, the mother of Jesus. Use the three-step LIP process like you did last week to uncover principles of encouragement. Read through the passage three times and follow these steps (I have done a few for you as examples):

Look for the facts. Don't make any interpretations here. Simply write what is happening in each verse.

Verse 39   Mary went to a town in Judah.

Verse 40   She entered Elizabeth's house

Verse 41

Verse 42

Verse 43

Verse 44

Verse 45

Interpret the meaning. Turn the lesson in the passage into a scriptural principle.

Verse 39   When we need encouragement, we must not be afraid to seek it out from godly people.

Verse 40   Go to a friend when you need your faith strengthened.

Verse 41

Verse 42

Verse 43

Verse 44

Verse 45

Pursue the application. Turn the principle you discovered into a personal question that applies the truth to your life.

Verse 39	When I need encouragement, do I seek it out? Or do I tend to wallow in self-pity?
Verse 40	Who are some friends that I can go to when I need to be strengthened?
Verse 41	
Verse 42	
Verse 43	
Verse 44	
Verse 45	

3. What key lesson did you learn today?

4. Write Ephesians 4:29 from memory.

Meaningful Makeover

Choose one question from those you posed in "Pursue the Application." Answer it honestly and come up with an action you can do to grow in that area. Use the space below or write in your journal.

Plump: Enlarge with Praise

Memory Verse

Let the one who boasts, boast in the Lord. 2 Corinthians 10:17

Plumping Products

Talk no more so very proudly, let not arrogance come from your mouth; for the LORD is a God of knowledge, and by Him actions are weighed. 1 Samuel 2:3

Full lips are all the rage. Movie stars and fashion models sport the plump lip look. Style magazines outline the steps to achieve the look of fuller lips. Some women even choose painful injections just to have a pretty pout. And if you're not willing to go through the twinge of the needle, a myriad of plumping products are available. Lip plumpers promise to boost your beauty.

At times, I am tempted to use another type of plumper: an image booster in the form of boasting. Instead of putting something on my lips to improve my outward appearance, I apply a little boastful speech to enhance the way you see me. Just a little bragging, a tad of flaunting, and a speck of self-important talk.

The application of this image plumper is usually not a conscious act. In fact, I try to avoid boastful talk. But watch out if I'm in a situation where I feel substandard. Suddenly, I'm pulling out the plumping agents.

Simple Tips for Fuller Lips

Besides using a lip-plumping product, there are some easy things you can do if you want your lips to appear fuller.

- Brush your lips: Gently brushing with a moistened toothbrush stimulates blood flow to your lips.

- Use a color trick: Try a lighter shade of lipstick on the bottom lip; lighter colors magnify.

- Be an illusionist: A dot of clear lip gloss over your lipstick in the center of your lips will reflect light, creating a 3-D effect.

Imagine you and I are introduced to each other at a gathering of successful and important people. Everyone in the crowd seems to hold an impressive position. Extraordinary accomplishments are discussed at every table. Suddenly, I feel inferior. I try to remedy that by letting it slip that I had three speaking engagements this week. (Layer 1 of the plumping agent.) Somehow I work it into the conversation that I am a published author. (Layer 2.) I mention a few of my recent accomplishments (more layers), and you begin to wonder how I even fit into the room with all those layers of pride.

Perhaps you, too, have used boost-your-own-image speech. Why do we do this? Why do we feel the need to brag?

If you had been listening to my attempt to make myself appear important, you might have thought I possessed an extra-large ego. Sometimes, this is the cause of boasting. We are proud of our accomplishments, and we want everyone to know about them. Self-adulation may indicate a very high opinion of oneself.

However, the opposite may also be true. In our fictional situation above, the reason I would have felt the need to pile on the plumping agent was insecurity. Hidden in my words was a need for approval.

Tips for Avoiding Boastful Speech

• Remember not to dominate conversations. Give others a chance to talk.

• Ask questions. After you have spoken about your interests, children, job, and so on, ask the other person about hers.

• Avoid comparisons. State your accomplishments and strengths matter-of-factly without comparing yourself to others.

• Observe your conversation partner's body language. If her eyes glaze over, it's time to change the subject!

Whether boasting is caused by an extra-large ego or a case of insecurity, the result is an attempt to enlarge one's self-image. How can we eliminate lip plumpers from our makeup bag?

God tells us in 1 Samuel 2:3, "Talk no more so very proudly, let not arrogance come from your mouth." God is commanding us not to talk proudly. No more boasting. No more bragging. No more flaunting.

We get the idea. God is not pleased with prideful talk, with arrogant speech. But what is our motivation to eliminate this kind of talk from our mouths? First Samuel 2:3 continues: "The LORD is a God of knowledge, and by Him actions are weighed."

I think we can look at this in two ways. One, I had better not boast because

God can see what I am doing. He will not be pleased with my prideful speech.

✝ *Applying the truth of God's love to my soul and allowing it to seep*
deep into my heart will do more for my self-image than
countless layers of boastful speech on my lips.

Two, I don't need to boast because God is a God of knowledge—He knows me! I don't have to run a Fortune 500 corporation to get His attention. He notices me even if I don't have a six-figure bank account or an important title. I don't have to bring a list of impressive accomplishments to God for Him to like me. I am precious to Him because I am His child.

A Word of Praise Today

I praise You, God, that I am precious to You, even though I may be insignificant in the eyes of the world. I praise You, God, for sending Your only Son for me.

What happens when we let that truth seep deep into our souls? We become less concerned with plumping up our image. We no longer feel the need to capture the attention of others.

Rejoice that you are known to God. Celebrate the fact that you do not have to shout above the noise to get Him to notice you. Delight in His love and mercy.

> *Father in heaven, You see me. You see me when I feel*
> *the need to wear layers of boastful speech. You see when*
> *I place more importance on the opinions of people than*
> *on Your gracious love. But because You see me through the*
> *righteousness of Christ, You forgive me for these sins. Help*
> *me to cherish Your grace and attention so I do not feel the*
> *need to boost my image. In Jesus' precious name. Amen.*

DAY 1

Lipstick Lesson

1. Full, pouty lips are in vogue. What is your take on this current trend and the lengths to which women go to achieve the look?

2. When are you tempted to boost your image? When you have received an honor? When your children or grandchildren have done something amazing? When you feel insecure? Talk about when and why you boast.

3. Read Psalm 52.

   a. David addresses this psalm to a "mighty man" (v. 1). Why might this type of person be more likely to use boastful speech?

   b. How does David describe the mouth of the boaster? (vv. 2–4)

   c. What did the boasting man do (v. 7)? How can this kind of behavior lead to bragging?

   d. In verses 8 and 9, David talks about his antidote for boasting. What things did he do differently than the boaster? How can these attitudes and actions eliminate the need for bragging?

4. What key lesson did you learn today?

5. Write out our memory verse for this week: "Let the one who boasts, boast in the Lord" (2 Corinthians 10:17).

Meaningful Makeover

Think about conversations you have had the past few days. Did you wear the lip plumper of boasting? Did you exhibit any of these plumping behaviors?

- Making myself the main topic of conversation
- Dropping names to impress people
- Using the suffixes *-er* and *-est* when talking about myself. (My work is better than hers. My daughter is the smartest in her class.)
- Not asking questions about the other person

Use the space below or write in your journal about your words. Confess and receive God's forgiveness. Write about what you can do to change your speech next time.

STEP 3

Outdo One Another

Love one another with brotherly affection. Outdo one another in showing honor. Romans 12:10

What do grandmothers like to brag about? Their grandchildren, of course! Grandmothers come armed with cute stories, amazing anecdotes, and—most certainly—brag books.

At one small group study I attended, the premeeting conversation centered on adorable grandbabies. One grandmother told how her son had taken his three-year-old daughter to see the town square decorated for Christmas. He pointed out the twinkling lights, the snow-flocked trees, and the horse-drawn carriages. When they had toured the whole square, the little girl said, "I want to see another square."

The father explained that there was only one town square. That precious three-year-old replied, "Then I want to see a triangle."

We all laughed at the cute story, but I immediately thought of my own brilliant grandson and my daughter's efforts to teach nineteen-month-old Aaron to read using flash cards. Not to be outdone, I told of how little Aaron was already able to read words like *square, triangle, parallelogram,* and *trapezoid.* Another woman in the group commented, "But he doesn't know what a trapezoid is."

"Oh, yes he does!" I informed her. "My daughter made yogurt Popsicles by putting strawberry yogurt into ice cube trays and sticking Popsicle sticks in. When they were frozen, she gave one to Aaron. After looking at it for a second, he said, 'Trapezoid.' If you think about it, the shape of a standard ice cube is a trapezoid."

I'm sure you will agree that my grandson is pretty amazing! But why did I feel the need to outdo the other grandmother's story? Why didn't I just enjoy the cute account of the town triangle?

Listen in on conversations and all around you, you will hear this need to be on top. One person tells about his trip to New York, another man jumps in to give a travelogue of his Mediterranean cruise. Before he is even finished, a woman begins a detailed account of her African safari.

This need to outdo one another is a form of bragging. When we feel that we need to "one-up" a friend, we are wearing a subtle shade of Boastful Burgundy. Why do we reach for this shade of speech? Why do we top another's statement with a grander one of our own?

Sometimes, we do this simply because we feel we are holding up our end of the conversation. We are adding more information to the topic being discussed.

So, what's wrong with one-upmanship?

- One-upmanship is a form of bragging.
- One-upmanship makes the other person feel inferior.
- One-upmanship does not display humility.

However, I realized that when people "one-upped" me, it made me feel second-rate. I felt that they didn't care enough about me to focus on my concerns or good fortune before immediately turning to their own problems or success. I realized that this game of one-upmanship was a way to appear superior.

Then I read Romans 12:10: "Love one another with brotherly affection. Outdo one another in showing honor." How are we supposed to outdo one another? In grabbing admiration for ourselves? In snatching all the attention?

No, we are to outdo one another in showing honor to others. We are to talk about their worth and merit. We are to shine the spotlight on our brothers and sisters in Christ instead of on ourselves.

☩ *When someone sings his own praises, he always gets the tune too high.*
Mary H. Waldrip[9]

What would it look like if I were trying to be the best in showing honor to others? Instead of jumping in with my own story after hearing a friend's tale, I would comment on her account. Perhaps ask a few questions. Find out her feelings about the incident.

If my friend shared a recent achievement, I would congratulate her and find out all the details rather than steal the limelight by immediately sharing my own good news. If my husband complained about his hectic day, I would resist the temptation to whine about my own horrific afternoon and instead listen empathetically. (Well, at least for a minute or two.)

In the Greek, the word translated outdo in Romans 12:10 is *proegeomai*, which means literally "to lead the way." But God does not want us to lead the way as if we were at the head of the parade in our honor. He wants us to excel—

to be the very best—at putting others first.

✝ *We should speak well of our neighbor, that is, we should praise our neighbor's good actions and qualities. (Luther's Small Catechism)*

If I'm truly attempting to outdo everyone else in showing honor and not receiving it, I will come alongside my friend instead of trying to leap ahead. I will prefer to listen than to talk. I will follow Paul's advice in Romans 12:15: "Rejoice with those who rejoice, weep with those who weep."

When Jesus walked on this earth, He was one of us, which means He could feel both our joys and sorrows; let us also try to walk in empathy with our brothers and sisters in Christ. Whether their road is paved with happiness or sorrow, let's take the time to listen as we walk beside them instead of jumping ahead with our own concerns. Throw out the tubes of Boastful Burgundy. Outdo one another in showing honor.

A Word of Praise for Today

Praise You, Jesus, for becoming one of us. You understand both our joys and our sorrows.

Dear humble Savior, thank You for your example of humility and empathy. Thank You for willingly coming into our world and feeling our joy and pain. Forgive me for times when I have been unwilling to do the same for the people in my life—even just for a moment. Help me to outdo others not in receiving honor, but in giving it in Your precious name. Amen.

DAY 2

Lipstick Lesson

1. Think of a time when you have been "one-upped"? How did you feel?

2. Romans 12:10 instructs us, "Outdo one another in showing honor." If you own several Bible versions or have access to an online Bible on the Internet, look up this verse in several translations and read how this verse is translated in each. Which is your favorite? Why?

3. Now put Romans 12:10 in context. Read Romans 12:9–21.

   a. Verse 11 says that we should "not be slothful in zeal" (ESV) or "not lagging behind in diligence" (NASB). What does this tell you about the work of honoring others?

   b. Verse 11 also instructs us to "serve the Lord." How are we serving the Lord when we honor others?

   c. Write down some specific ways we can "outdo one another in showing honor" according to verses 12–21.

4. What key lesson did you learn today?

5. Write out our memory verse for this week: "Let the one who boasts, boast in the Lord" (2 Corinthians 10:17).

Meaningful Makeover

Choose one of the specific ways to show honor that you discovered in Romans 12:21 (Question 3c above) to implement this week. Write who you will honor and how.

DAY 3

A Better Way to Boast

I will boast all the more gladly of my weaknesses, so that the power of Christ may rest upon me. 2 Corinthians 12:9b "What is your greatest weakness?"

My son, Nathaniel, has been asked this question many times in the past year. You see, like thousands of other college graduates, he was on the quest for a job. Prospective employers love to pull out this question to catch the interviewee off guard.

Experts advise answering this difficult question by describing a weakness you discovered in a previous job and how you overcame it. (I used to be disorganized, but I have found a way to prioritize my tasks.) Or you could tell about a weakness you have that is not at all related to the job you are applying for. (I am addicted to Rocky Road ice cream.)

But what if you gave a brutally honest answer to this question like:

"Truthfully? My greatest weakness is probably my lazy streak. I need a lot of outside motivation to get my work done."

"My greatest weakness is my tendency to question authority."

"My greatest weakness? That would have to be my propensity to oversleep and be late for work."

Career coaches would definitely not advise any of those answers. To effectively land a job, you must wear just enough lip plumper to show off your strengths honestly without appearing conceited.

The Proper Way to Brag

At times, it is necessary to tell others about ourselves to advance our business or land a job. How can we promote ourselves without obnoxious bragging? Here are a few tips:

- Don't give a laundry list of accomplishments—focus on one or two.

- Don't compare yourself to others—state the facts succinctly.

- Don't be overbearing—talk in a conversational manner.

- Don't exaggerate—stick to the truth.

- Don't look stern or aloof—instead look positive and enthusiastic.

How far would the apostle Paul get in today's job market? He told the people of Corinth, "I will boast all the more gladly of my weaknesses" (2 Corinthians 12:9). A career coach would probably not encourage this approach in a job interview, but it turns out that this is exactly what God recommends for our lives.

I admit that this goes against my every natural inclination. I am more comfortable telling you about my talents and hiding my deficiencies. And yet, God tells me that wearing a lip plumper isn't all bad if I'm using it to brag about my frailty instead of my strength.

Look at Paul's statement again:

> But He said to me, "My grace is sufficient for you, for My power is made perfect in weakness." Therefore I will boast all the more gladly of my weaknesses, so that the power of Christ may rest upon me. For the sake of Christ, then, I am content with weaknesses, insults, hardships, persecutions, and calamities. For when I am weak, then I am strong.
> 2 Corinthians 12:9–10

Paul made a profound first point: God is enough.

Although we want to brag about what we have accomplished on our own, God wants us to experience what His strength accomplishes through us. I have experienced this truth as a public speaker. God exhibited His sense of humor in calling me to be a Christian speaker. I certainly would not have picked this shy, insecure person out of a crowd to get up and speak. For one thing, I probably would not have even been in the crowd, but home alone reading a book!

When a representative of a Christian ministry suggested I become one of their speakers, I thought, *Yeah, right.* I wouldn't have even considered it if my mother hadn't stepped in and asked that more information be sent to me.

Although I now love speaking to women's groups about Christ's love and grace, I still do not consider it my natural strength. I need to practice a lot before a speech feels comfortable to me. When it comes down to being an excellent speaker, I do not have what it takes.

But God does.

And if I had never accepted the challenge to step behind a podium, I might never have discovered God's power is such an amazing way. We do not discover the sufficiency of God's strength until we recognize the insufficiency of our own.

STEP 3

> ✝ *The best way to discover the sufficiency of God's strength is to admit the insufficiency of my own.*

The second point of Paul's statement is: As I boast about my weaknesses, God's power rests on me.

When I first began telling my faith story at luncheons and banquets, I was so unsure of myself that I physically hung onto that podium. I was certain my message was falling flat and was ineffective. But when women came up to me afterward to tell me that my message brought them closer to God, I was truly surprised. I had no problem attributing any success to God's power; certainly shaky knees were a sign of my own weakness.

A Word of Praise for Today

Praise You, Lord, for Your mighty and potent power, sufficient for every need.

The third point in our focus verse is: Because of Jesus, we can be content with our weaknesses.

The word for content in the Greek is *eudokeo*, which means "to think something is good or to choose something." Paul is saying that he willingly chooses to be weak, that he is glad he is weak, because then he can rely on Christ's strength.

I have also learned to be glad about my weakness. My meager natural talent as a speaker forces me to spend a lot of time in preparation and prayer, both of which have drawn me closer to God. If I were innately good at speaking, I might be satisfied to rely on my own strength instead of God's. That's a little like relying on the power of a garden spade when a backhoe is available.

So what would you say if God were interviewing you for a job? Would you tout your ability and talk up your strength? Or would you admit your limitations honestly and receive His power to complete the work? Let's wear just enough lip plumper to boast about our weaknesses. Let's experience God's sufficiency and strength.

Almighty God, I would rather appear strong than expose my flaws. But I want to experience the sufficiency of

Your strength and I know that the only way to do that is admit the insufficiency of my own. Help me to willingly boast about my weakness so I can experience Your power. In Jesus' name. Amen.

STEP 3

DAY 3

Lipstick Lesson

1. How would you respond to the question: "What is your greatest weakness?" How does it feel to talk about your flaws or limitations?

2. In 2 Corinthians 12:9, we read Paul's statement: "I will boast all the more gladly of my weaknesses." Let's examine this passage in context to see how Paul was able to do this. Read 2 Corinthians 11:16–12:10.

   a. In 2 Corinthians 12:6, Paul says, "Though if I should wish to boast, I would not be a fool, for I would be speaking the truth." Why does Paul have a right to boast?

   b. In 12:7, Paul talks about a "thorn . . . in the flesh." No one knows what this thorn is, although it is usually thought to be some kind of chronic health problem. How can a weakness actually be helpful to us?

   c. Can you think of a time when a weakness of yours turned out to be a benefit?

   d. In verse 9, Paul talks about grace. Grace not only turns us to Christ, but continues to strengthen us in the Christian faith. What is the relationship between our weakness and God's grace?

4. What key lesson did you learn today?

5. Write out our memory verse for this week: "Let the one who boasts, boast in the Lord" (2 Corinthians 10:17).

Meaningful Makeover

Today, journal about one of your perceived weaknesses. Think about how that frailty may actually help you in your relationship with God. Take the bold step of thanking Him for your weakness and boasting about it to others.

DAY 4

Make God's Day

I will bless the LORD at all times;
His praise shall continually be in my mouth.

My soul makes its boast in the LORD;
let the humble hear and be glad. Psalm 34:1–2

I used to love going to the grocery store down the street from my house. But not for the reason you might think. Yes, I enjoyed the yeasty smell of the bakery. And I got a little thrill when picking out a new ice cream flavor.

However, the real reason I liked going to this particular grocery store was in the produce section. For among the shiny red apples and crisp green lettuce was a smiling produce manager. And whenever I walked into the store with my preteen daughter, he would say something like, "Well, if it isn't the two sisters again!" Now, I knew that he knew that I was Anna's mother, but because he always gave this you-don't-look-your-age compliment with such a friendly smile, I always left that store with a little more joy in my heart to go along with the food in my grocery sacks.

Alas, that store closed and I no longer can get a compliment along with my strawberries. But my experience there came to mind as I was contemplating the subject of praise. I was pondering why God wants us to praise Him. After all, He already knows that He is holy, all-powerful, majestic, omniscient, wise, good, and loving. Why does He want us to tell Him so?

Then I thought of how I felt after my trip to the grocery store. Those little flattering words made my day and lifted my spirits. I began to wonder if that's what words of admiration do for God too. Maybe words of praise from His daughter gladden His heart.

✝ *Make God's day. Praise Him for who He is.*

Too often, my prayers are simply lists of things I want. Sometimes, I also remember to thank Him for blessings I have already received. But by praising God, it shows that I value Him for who He is and not only for what He can do for me. Praise acknowledges God as a Person to be appreciated, a Sovereign Be-

76

ing to be worshiped and not simply a genie to do my bidding.

King David was an expert in praise. In Psalm 34:1–3, he wrote:

> I will bless the LORD at all times;
> His praise shall continually be in my mouth.
>
> My soul makes its boast in the LORD;
> let the humble hear and be glad.
>
> Oh, magnify the LORD with me,
> and let us exalt His name together!

David praised God "at all times." He not only glorified God in periods of joy; he worshiped Him in times of sadness. This particular psalm was written after he had escaped from the king of Gath without harm, but David also praised God when he was in danger. He recognized that although circumstances may change, God remained the same. The Lord was still his rock, his refuge, his redeemer.

David's soul made "its boast in the LORD." King David had a pretty exciting life. He could have written a best-seller bragging about his encounters with wild lions and giants, but instead he wrote songs honoring God. As humans, our pride and boasting often get in the way of our relationships with God and men. But when we boast in the Lord and praise His name, that pride dissolves. Michael Youssef, in his book, *Empowered by Praise*, asserts that pride cannot keep company with praise, for one will surely push the other aside.[10]

David urges us to "magnify the Lord." To magnify is to make something appear larger. God's character does not change through praise; He has always been and always will be almighty, omniscient, and powerful. But when we worship God, He becomes larger in our own eyes because we recognize Him for who He is.

The ABCs of Praising God

Use the alphabet to praise God for who He is. Here are a few to get you started.

A	Abba, Father	N	Near
B	Beginning and End	O	Omniscient
C	Comforter	P	Powerful
D	Defender	Q	Quieter of my soul
E	Everlasting	R	Redeemer
F	Faithful	S	Savior

G	Generous	T	True
H	Holy	U	Unchanging
I	Immortal	V	Victorious
J	Just	W	Worthy
K	Kind	X	Xtra strong
L	Loving	Y	Yesterday and today the same
M	Majestic	Z	Zealous

One tool I have found helpful in worshiping God for His character is praising through the alphabet. King David, in fact, used this technique in Psalm 34. It is an acrostic poem where each verse begins with a successive letter of the Hebrew alphabet. Our own English alphabet helps me focus on God's nature. During my time of worship, I praise God for attributes that begin with each letter of the alphabet. For instance, "I praise You, God, for Your Almighty power, I marvel in Your Beauty, and I am moved by Your Compassion."

This technique prevents my mind from wandering back to my to-do list when I truly want to be concentrating on God. It helps me to be creative as I strive to find new attributes of God each time I go through the alphabet. I can use this method of praise on my walk around the neighborhood or in the middle of the night when I can't fall back to asleep.

A Word of Praise for Today

I praise You, God, for You are the great Artist of creation, the Balm for my soul, the Calm in my storm, and the Desire of my heart.

Praising God for His character enables me to know God in a deeper way. It strengthens my faith as I concentrate on His goodness and strength. So today join me in praising God. Tell Him He is awesome. Rave over His wisdom. Compliment Him on His goodness.

Make His day.

DAY 4

Lipstick Lesson

1. How do you feel when you receive a compliment? Use those emotions to imagine how praise might affect God.

2. David wrote, "My soul makes its boast in the LORD" (Psalm 34:2). What has God done for you lately that you could boast about?

3. Read Psalm 145.

   a. To praise God is to worship Him for His character. Write down some of God's attributes that you find in this psalm.

   b. Write your own little psalm using the attributes of God that mean the most to you today.

4. What key lesson did you learn today?

5. Write out our memory verse for this week.

Meaningful Makeover

Take some time today to praise God through the alphabet. Use your journal to write out your praises or to describe your worship experience. Which of God's attributes is most meaningful to you right now? What emotions did you experience during your praise time?

DAY 5

Facebook Friends and Twitter Followers

Perceiving then that they were about to come and take Him by force to make Him king, Jesus withdrew again to the mountain by Himself. John 6:15

"Come on, let's get out of this crowd and get something to eat," the VIP shouted over his shoulder. Pete, his assistant, nodded. He called out to the rest of their entourage and they shouldered their way through the crowd to a nearby boat that was advertising a short cruise to a remote destination.

Their little group settled on the deck of the boat, relieved to be out of the crush of the crowd. It had been like this for months. People everywhere were clamoring to see their leader, an acclaimed teacher. Pete took his cell phone out of his pocket, ready to tweet about this latest crowd, but saw his leader shake his head and motion for Pete to put it away. "Not now," the teacher said. "Let's just relax."

The gentle rocking of the boat calmed their frazzled nerves. But the reprieve didn't last long. As soon as the boat docked and they stepped onto the shore, Pete noticed a group of people in the distance. Evidently, the crowd they had been trying to escape had followed them on foot along the shore.

Pete looked at the VIP. Yes, he had seen the approaching crowd too. Although he looked exhausted, Pete knew the great teacher would never turn them away. The master sat down on a hill and slowly the crowd grew. And grew. Pete did a quick estimate: at least five thousand people had gathered there in the middle of nowhere!

The great teacher gently instructed them about life and love, and the people hung on his every word. Soon it was late afternoon, and Pete's rumbling stomach reminded him they had not eaten. Most likely, every stomach in the crowd was feeling the same empty gnawing. But obviously there were no McDonald's or Wendy's nearby.

Just then, he heard the teacher ask Phil, another member of their group, where they could get some food for the people who had come to hear him speak. Phil laughed and said that even if they had thousands of dollars it wouldn't be enough to buy each person a bite of food.

Andy spoke up, "I already checked around." (Evidently, his stomach was growling too.) "The only food in the crowd is a few tuna sandwiches in one kid's lunch."

The VIP said, "Bring it here."

The master opened the lunch sack and prayed a blessing. He reached into the sack and pulled out some of the food, handing it to his friends to distribute it. Each time he put his hand in the bag, there were more sandwiches. Pete couldn't figure it out. Soon everyone had eaten, not just a bite, but enough to make them lay down on the grass, drowsy with satisfaction.

Pete pulled out his smart phone again. He had to tweet about this. No one had ever seen anything like this before! Imagine the publicity. News crews pulling up with satellite dishes and microphones. Cameras flashing. His teacher would now become world famous!

But before Pete could tap out the message on his phone, his leader had taken it from his hand, put it in his pocket and walked away.

What if Jesus lived on earth today? How many Facebook friends would He have? How many Twitter followers?

As I pictured what the feeding of the five thousand might have been like had it happened today, I couldn't help but think that the disciples probably would have been urging Jesus to update His Facebook status: "Fed five thousand people with five loaves of bread and two fish." They might have acted as agents for million-dollar book deals. They could have sought out marketing experts. And Jesus would have taken advantage of every opportunity, because who wouldn't want all that attention—right?

Wrong.

The Gospel of John tells us that after the miraculous picnic the people "were about to come and take Him by force to make Him king" (John 6:15) and Jesus knew it. He could have garnered plenty of attention and acclaim. But instead He walked away.

> ✝ *He who is humble is confident and wise.*
> *He who brags is insecure and lacking. Lisa Edmondson*[11]

Why? What can we learn from Jesus about boasting and seeking attention?

Jesus didn't view people as potential fans. He didn't count the crowd in order to boost His ego. Mark 6:34 says that Jesus "saw a great crowd, and He had compassion on them, because they were like sheep without a shepherd." He looked inside people's hearts, perceived their needs, and met them before tending to His own.

Instead of boasting about His ability to multiply food and so attract attention for Himself, Jesus saw the crowd as an opportunity to serve. Instead of adding the event to His résumé, He simply met the needs of the people. He healed the sick, nourished souls, and filled stomachs.

Jesus didn't seek earthly acclaim. The people wanted to make Him king, but rather than claiming the status they were offering, Jesus walked away. Matthew's account tells us "He went up on the mountain by Himself to pray" (Matthew 14:23). Instead of worldly fame, Jesus sought the approval of His Father.

> ✝ *Live for the Father's approval instead of the world's.*

Looking at Jesus' example, I am convicted. Too often, I seek occasions to attract attention instead of opportunities to serve. I am tempted to view people as a means to get what I want instead of looking empathetically at their needs. I can get trapped by the desire for fame and success and forget that the Father's approval is all that really matters.

A Word of Praise for Today

Praise You, Jesus, that You fill the gnawing of my empty soul.

Jesus reminds me that He is able to meet all my needs. Just as He filled the thousands of gnawing stomachs that day so long ago, He fills my empty soul at His Holy Table. I don't have to wear the lip plumper of boasting to gain His approval. He is able to fill me with the fullness of His love so that, in turn, I can see others with eyes of compassion. People are not just Facebook friends or Twitter followers. They are opportunities for me to serve in the love of Christ.

Jesus, miraculous Provider, forgive me when I have looked at Your people as only a way for me to gain attention and approval. Thank You for Your example of shunning the attention of this world and seeking the approval of the Father. Help me to follow in Your steps and view my brothers and sisters in Christ with Your eyes of compassion. In Your precious name. Amen.

DAY 5

Lipstick Lesson

1. Are you on Facebook or Twitter? Talk about the advantages and disadvantages of social media.

2. What is your reaction to the modern adaptation of the feeding of the five thousand story? What do you think would happen if a miracle like that happened today?

3. LIP Study. This week, let's take a closer look at John's account of the feeding of the five thousand. Read John 6:1–15 and use the three-step LIP approach to uncover lessons about Jesus' attitude toward people.

Look for the facts. Don't make any interpretations here. Simply write what is happening in each verse.

Verse 1 Jesus crossed to the far shore of the Sea of Galilee.

Verse 2 A great crowd of people followed Him because they saw the miraculous healings He had done.

Verse 3 Jesus went up on a mountainside and sat down with His disciples.

Verse 4 The Jewish Passover was near.

Verse 5

Verse 6

Verse 7

Verse 8

Verse 9

Verse 10

Verse 11

Verse 12

Verse 13

Verse 14

Verse 15

Interpret the meaning. Turn the lesson in the passage into a scriptural principle.

Verse 1 At times, we need to get away by ourselves.

Verse 2 People are attracted by the work of God.

Verse 3 We need to spend time with supportive people.

Verse 4 Okay, this is a tough one. One commentator conjectured that John included this fact because the people knew that Jesus would be going to Jerusalem for the Passover and therefore this would be their last chance to see Him for awhile.[12] A lesson we can glean from this fact is that we should be diligent to take advantage of every opportunity to spend time with Christ.

Verse 5

Verse 6

Verse 7

Verse 8

Verse 9

Verse 10

Verse 11

Verse 12

Verse 13

Verse 14

Verse 15

Pursue the application. Turn the principle you discovered into a personal question that applies the truth to your life.

Verse 1 When could I set up a time for a private retreat?

Verse 2 What has God done for me lately that I can tell others about?

Verse 3 Who are the supportive people in my life that I need to meet with regularly?

Verse 4 Have I been neglecting church or Bible study?

Verse 5

Verse 6

Verse 7

Verse 8

Verse 9

Verse 10

Verse 11

Verse 12

Verse 13

Verse 14

Verse 15

4. What key lesson did you learn today?

5. Write out 2 Corinthians 10:17 from memory.

Meaningful Makeover

Choose one question from those you posed in "Pursue the Application." In the space below or in your journal, write your honest answer to this question and come up with an action you can do to grow in that area.

Line:
Speak with Truth

Memory Verse

Whoever of you loves life and desires to see many good days, keep your tongue from evil and your lips from speaking lies.
Psalm 34:12–13 NIV

DAY 1

A Terrible Liar

Whoever of you loves life and desires to see many good days, keep your tongue from evil and your lips from speaking lies.
Psalm 34:12–13 NIV

I'm a terrible liar. Honest.

It's not that I do it a lot; it's that I can't seem to do it at all. Probably this is because I am actually very good at something else.

Blushing.

This was especially true in my youth. The instant I would try to concoct an untruth, redness did not simply creep up my face, it ran, rushed, raced. My normally pale, white skin was suddenly tomato red.

This automatic color change is so perturbing. I hate it. Yet it has served me well in the area of honesty.

Honesty is the foundation of a Mouth Makeover, just as lip liner is the base of any good lip look. I used to skip this step in my makeup routine, but I have learned that lip liner, when properly applied, can help your lipstick from bleeding into the fine lines around your mouth and help the color last longer. It will make your lipstick stick.

Truth will make your words stick. Without it, family members will be skeptical of your statements. Co-workers will question your reports. Friends will doubt your promises.

The Proper Way to Apply Lip Liner

1. Using a soft lip pencil, outline the V-shaped curve in the center of your upper lip. Draw the line directly on the edge of your lip.

2. Using short, feathering strokes, go outward from the V-shaped curve to each outer corner.

3. On your lower lip, draw a line from the outer corners to the center using those same small strokes.

4. Fill in the lip from the outline to the center of the lip.
   This will help your lipstick adhere and prevent that
   telltale "ghost line" when your lipstick starts to wear off.

Author Phil Callaway admits that truth-telling is difficult for him. In fact, for one year it was a literal challenge. Callaway's editor called him up one day and asked him to write a book about telling the absolute truth for one year. Initially, the idea of writing this book didn't appeal to Callaway because he confesses that he has a habit of embellishing the facts. Partly this is because he is a Christian humorist and although the stories he tells are 99¾ percent true, he adds just enough fiction to draw a bigger laugh.

Despite his reluctance, Callaway took the dare and his book *To Be Perfectly Honest* chronicles his year of complete candor. Some days the truth test was trouble-free and his entries read something like, "Not much to say. Was completely truthful and didn't even cringe."

However, most days his efforts in truth-telling were complicated. On day seven, Callaway was stumped when his mother-in-law asked if he'd like to come over for supper. Hmmm . . . *like* to come over? How could he answer that honestly?

Conversations with his wife proved to be problematic too. What if his wife asked, "Dear, does this outfit make me look fat?" [13]

When I read Callaway's journal of attempting perfect honesty, I realized that I also stretch the truth occasionally. So I might be better at lying than I want to admit.

For instance, I'm late for an appointment and I apologize, saying, "The traffic was terrible and, wouldn't you know, I had to stop for a train." I did have to wait for a train—but it was a short one. The real reason I was late was that I lost track of time surfing the Web. I tell a half-truth.

"That outfit looks fantastic on you!" I gush at the woman behind the counter. Actually, the color she is wearing is not very attractive on her, but I want to return a purchase and I have lost the receipt. I use a little flattery.

How about you? Would you take the challenge of living completely truthfully for a year?

Types of Lies

Falsehoods can be grouped into the following categories:

- White Lies—telling a little untruth to avoid hurting a friend
- Flattery—dishonest communication to gain something for yourself
- Exaggeration—stretching the truth to make yourself look good
- Half-truths—leaving out key facts
- Deceit—falsifying forms or information to your advantage

Of course, some people will argue that there are only two types of lies: the ones you get away with and the ones you get caught telling!

In case you need a little motivation for eliminating lies and deceit from your vocabulary, let's look at our memory verse for this week:

> Whoever of you loves life and desires to see many good days,
> keep your tongue from evil and your lips from speaking lies.
> (Psalm 34:12–13 NIV)

What can we learn about lying and truth-telling from these verses? First of all, this verse informs us that lying is evil. When God issued the command, "Keep your tongue from evil," He spelled out one specific way to do this—don't lie! In his Small Catechism, Martin Luther wrote, "God forbids us to tell lies about our neighbor in a court of law or elsewhere, that is, to lie about, lie to, or withhold the truth from our neighbor" (Luther's Small Catechism).

God's Law shows us our sin. The Bible contains stories about God's harsh punishments for liars. You might remember the Old Testament story of Gehazi, who was penalized with leprosy for lying about some gifts he took from a visitor (2 Kings 5). In the New Testament, Ananias and Sapphira were struck down dead for dishonesty concerning some land they had sold (Acts 5:1–10).

God's obvious hatred for lying should be enough to make us practice honesty, but if we need more motivation, we only need to realize that dishonesty kills our human relationships. Just ask any woman who has been lied to repeatedly by her husband. Look at the parents who find out their teenage son has been deceiving them about his after-school activities. Lies crush trust.

Second, Psalm 34:11–14 tells us that truth is a key ingredient to loving your life. King David says, "Hey, if you want to wake up every day with a passion for life, watch what you say. And especially stop lying through your teeth."

A Word of Truth for Today

Because of Jesus' sacrifice, God invites me to approach Him honestly and openly.

Learning to be open and honest with yourself, with the people in your life, and with God can bring profound joy and peace. It is refreshing to share your heart openly without trying to pretend you are someone you are not. Honest speech leads to a full life.

This week, we will explore more about truth. Although I sometimes skip the step of lip liner in my makeup routine, I cannot neglect truth in my everyday speech. Because of my built-in lie detector, I thought this step would be an easy one for me. But God showed me that although my talent for blushing may have prevented me from telling whoppers to others, at times, I have not been totally honest in His presence. As I dove into God's Word, He taught me about speaking the truth in love and the importance of authenticity. Let's learn how to use the lip liner of truth correctly.

> *Father, Your Word tells me You despise lying. Although I know this, I am still tempted to be dishonest in order to shift the blame or get what I want. Help me to live honestly and transparently with You and the people around me. In Jesus' name. Amen.*

STEP 4

DAY 1

Lipstick Lesson

1. Today we talked about lip liner and speaking truth. Discuss the benefits of each.

2. The sidebar on page 90 listed five types of lies.

    a. List any other types of lies you can think of.

    b. Of all the lies, which do you think are the most hurtful?

3. Read the story of Ananias and Sapphira in Acts 5:1–10.

    a. What was the lie that they both told?

    b. What was their punishment?

    c. In verse 4, Peter told Ananias that he had not only lied to men, but also to God. Do you think God views all lies this way? Why or why not?

    d. Why do you think Ananias and Sapphira decided to tell this lie? (Reading Acts 4:32–35 may provide insight.)

    e. Why are we sometimes tempted to lie?

4. What key lesson did you learn today?

5. Write out our memory verse for this week: "Whoever of you loves life and desires to see many good days, keep your tongue from evil and your lips from speaking lies" (Psalm 34:12–13 NIV). To help you memorize this passage, write it out in the space below.

Meaningful Makeover

Think about what came out of your mouth in the past week. Did you tell any half-truths? use a little flattery? cover up your true feelings? Spend some time writing, here or in your journal, about your words and examine why you may have spoken dishonestly. Confess and receive God's forgiveness.

DAY 2

Truth in the Inner Being

Behold, You delight in truth in the inward being, and You teach me wisdom in the secret heart. Psalm 51:6

Truth in the inward being.

Honesty in the deep recesses of your soul.

Openness in the secret places of your heart.

What emotions spring to mind when you read those phrases? Relief? Peace? Intrigue? Terror? All of the above?

I admit to feeling a little of each. I'm intrigued by the idea of being completely open to someone. Often, I hold a part of myself back, afraid of unveiling all my hopes or exposing all my failures. Maybe without the tension of gripping my heart tightly shut, I would feel a great sense of relief. Yet the thought of opening up my soul so freely is also terrifying. For my failures could be condemned. My hopes could be smashed into tiny shards of despair.

So I am hesitant to show anyone the deep places of my soul. I'm reluctant to be completely honest with anyone, even God.

Come As You Are

When I was a little girl, we always dressed up for church. My mother made sure I had a pretty dress and patent leather shoes to wear on Sunday. We wanted to look our best for God.

Today, churches encourage us to "come as you are." Yet sometimes when I go to God in prayer, I still think I have to approach Him in my Sunday best. I feel I have to look pretty, not dirty. Perfect, not broken.

But when I read the Book of Psalms, I see that God actually welcomes absolute honesty and brokenness. The psalmists poured out their not-so-pretty emotions, their desperate fears, and their broken hearts. If God didn't like those kinds of prayers, I don't think He would have included them in His Word. God invites us to come as we are.

But it says right there in the Bible: God delights in truth in the inner being. He desires integrity, sincerity, transparency. As I contemplated this, I felt a nudge from God to take time for truth. I had an idea to set aside some time to allow God to show me the reality of my soul. I figured this was God's idea because I am much more of a doer than a sit-and-listener. So one morning I sat down with my Bible and a few blank pieces of paper. I reread David's words, "Behold, You delight in truth in the inward being" (Psalm 51:6) and prayed that God would show me the truth of what was in my heart. As I entered into this time of listening, I expected to hear where I had strayed from God's path. After all, David wrote Psalm 51 after Nathan had confronted him about his affair with Bathsheba. David had been ignoring his wrongdoing in this whole mess, and God wanted to show him an accurate picture of his soul.

As I sat still before God, I remembered times in the past week when my behavior and attitudes were less than stellar. On one sheet of paper, I wrote down the things that came to mind:

- Snippy attitude with my husband
- Neglect of my quiet time yesterday
- Putting my wants above others' needs

Those were no surprise. I had already been berating myself for those misdeeds. Thirty imaginary lashes on my back.

But as I sat there, other things began to bubble to the surface. Attitudes that were there all along, but, like David, I had not recognized them as sin:

- Trepidation about the future
- Fear of failure
- Anxiety about my work

God had seen those attitudes all along, of course, but I was too busy to notice them. And if I was aware of a twinge of worry or a shiver of dread, I did not call it sin. Yet what is anxiety or fear but a demonstration of a lack of trust in God's provision and plan?

During my "truth time," I also expected God to shine His spotlight into the closet of my heart where I stored my longings and desires. Another verse from the Psalms had been rolling around in my mind: "O Lord, all my longing is before You; my sighing is not hidden from You" (Psalm 38:9). God obviously knew what my heart yearned for. And, of course, I was aware of my surface desires: Food. Water. Chocolate. Family. Friends. Chocolate. Rest. Sleep. Chocolate.

But often fulfilling those surface cravings doesn't actually satisfy me because there are deeper needs that are left unmet. So I asked God to show me some of those deeper needs and I wrote them on another sheet of paper. Some of them were big and nebulous; others more immediate and practical:

- To make a difference with my life
- A mission or cause to work for besides my local church
- Recognition of my work
- More time with friends
- A more productive work routine

Writing down all of those desires helped cleanse me of worry. Stored in the closet of my heart, those cravings brought fear that they might never be fulfilled. But by bringing them into the open, by being honest with myself, I saw that God could easily manage all those longings. All could be met in God's sufficiency. I like what author Richard Foster says: confession ends our game of charades. When we appear unmasked before God, He loves us as we are and transforms our hearts.[14]

Sins confessed. Desires uncovered. These two elements alone would have made my "truth time" successful. But a surprising thing happened as I sat there listening to God's voice: He offered a third category of truth. I sensed Him whispering, "Wait a minute, Sharla. You are forgetting the truth of how I see you." On a third sheet of paper, I wrote what He put into my heart:

- You are My child.
- When I look at you, I see a precious daughter.
- My grace through Christ has made you clean.
- I have amazing gifts planned for you—just wait and see.

The truth of God's love and grace through Christ washed over me. I felt led to destroy the list of sins and the page of longings. God had already reassured me that He had done away with the first list—I was covered with His grace. He helped me to see that He would take care of the second list—He only asked me to trust His timing. It was the truth of the third list that I needed to hang onto—God's love and grace are all I need.

A Word of Truth for Today

God's grace fills the corners of my heart, erasing my sin and fulfilling my desires.

Truth in the inward being. At first, that phrase sounded terrifying. But letting go of my death grip on the door to my soul brought release and peace. My failures were condemned as sin, but then forgiven by a loving Savior. My dreams were not shattered, but nurtured with hope. Opening up the secret places of my heart allowed God to fill them with His grace.

God of grace, thank You for allowing me to come to You broken and needy. You desire truth in the inner being and that gets a little messy at times. But honesty in Your presence is a cleansing tool. The truth of Your grace washes my soul and fills every secret corner of my heart. Thank You, Lord. In Jesus' name. Amen.

STEP 4

DAY 2

Lipstick Lesson

1. What emotions do you feel when you read these phrases?

    Truth in the inward being

    Honesty in the deep recesses of your soul

    Openness in the secret places of your heart

2. Look up the following verses and write down the truth of how God sees you:

    a. Psalm 139:14

    b. Song of Solomon 4:7

    c. Isaiah 43:1

    d. Isaiah 43:4

    e. 1 John 3:1

    f. How can these truths help you grow in faith?

3. What key lesson did you learn today?

4. Write out our memory verse for this week: "Whoever of you loves life and desires to see many good days, keep your tongue from evil and your lips from speaking lies" (Psalm 34:12–13 NIV). Read a phrase, then cover it and write it. Recite as much of the verse as you can without looking.

Meaningful Makeover

I encourage you to take a "truth time." Meditate on Psalm 51:6: "Behold, You delight in truth in the inward being, and You teach me wisdom in the secret heart." Ask God to show you the truth of what is in your heart. Take note of His whispers of how He sees you. Write about the experience of truth in the inward being.

"I'm fine"

*Do not lie to one another, seeing that you have put off the
old self with its practices and have put on the new self, which
is being renewed in knowledge after the image of its creator.
Colossians 3:9–10*

"Hi, Erika! Great to see you. How are you?" I greeted my friend as she walked into our Toastmasters meeting.

"I'm fine." Erika's ordinarily smiling face was locked in a frown. Her usually enthusiastic tone of voice was transformed to one flat note.

Call me exceptionally perceptive, but I wasn't buying Erika's words. It turned out that Erika had just experienced a disappointment. But although she was bummed, my bubbly and energetic friend tried to sound upbeat.

How many times have you responded "I'm fine" when your heart was actually aching? How often have you pasted on a smile when you didn't want others to see your pain?

Granted, the question "How are you?" has become a standard greeting in our culture. I'm not going to tell the dentist's receptionist my list of aches and pains. The grocery store clerk doesn't want to hear the complete saga of my virus-plagued kids throwing up all night. So I respond with the expected response, "I'm fine" and get on with my day.

Safe Authenticity

We cannot open up and share honest feelings with every person we meet. Our friends and acquaintances are not all on the same level of intimacy. Not everyone is trustworthy. Here are some questions to ask yourself before you share your heart:

• Does this person demonstrate authenticity? If she has shared her own insecurities, you are probably safe in sharing yours.

• Has this person gossiped to me about others? If so, you can be pretty sure she will also share your secrets.

- Does this person demonstrate a judgmental attitude?
  Don't set yourself up for condemnation.

But too often we also do this with close friends. I may repeat the words "I'm fine" when I am actually worried about my mother's health, depressed about my son's lack of job prospects, or fearful about an upcoming medical test. I don't want to appear vulnerable. Besides, I'm a Christian, right? I'm supposed to be confident in the Lord. If I admit my fear or sadness, will my friends think I'm not a very good Christian?

Attempting to project a certain image has also prevented me from admitting my flaws. If disclosing my vulnerability is uncomfortable, confessing my imperfections is terrifying. So when someone asks me "How are you?" I'm tempted to say, "I've been really busy." See how important I am. I might reply, "I'm doing great—working on a new book!" See how successful I am. Or I may say, "Things are good. I've been doing a lot of work at church lately." See how spiritual I am.

✝ *Be who you is, cause if you ain't who you is, then you is who you ain't.*
Harry Hein[15]

However, a more honest answer might be "I'm really missing my grandkids in China." But that would show how lonely I am. Or, "I'm a little frustrated. My writing hasn't been going that well lately." But that would show how ineffective I am. Or, "I'm struggling with jealousy." But, heavens, that would show how human I am!

Authenticity scares us. So we tend to dab on a mask like we apply our makeup. We cover up mistakes like we conceal blemishes. We plump up our accomplishments like we enhance our smiles with lipstick.

But what does God tell us about honesty? Colossians 3:9–10 says:

> Do not lie to one another, seeing that you have put off the old
> self with its practices and have put on the new self, which is
> being renewed in knowledge after the image of its creator.

God commands us to practice honesty with one another. Of course, this means avoiding lying, deceit, and general fibbing, but I think at the root of this our Father is also telling us, "Don't try to be someone you are not. Do try to be the person I called you to be."

A Word of Truth for Today

The Father is shaping me to look like His Son. In Christ, I can be a righteous and authentic version of myself.

In Colossians, Paul tells us that we are able to do this because we have taken off our old self—the old self that needed to impress others, put on airs, and look good at all costs. The new self is authentic, because the honest truth is that our new image is the image of our Creator. Romans 8:29 tells us we are "conformed to the image of His Son." When God looks at us, He doesn't see the mess that we sometimes see in the mirror. He sees us looking like Jesus—covered with His holiness.

A ssessing Your Authenticity

To begin to live without daily dabbing on a mask, try asking yourself these questions:

- Do I try to convince others that I am better than I really am?

- Am I reluctant to admit a mistake for fear I will look bad?

- Am I too proud to ask for help?

- Do I exaggerate a story to make my life sound more interesting?

- Did I do something in private today that I would be afraid to admit in public?

- Am I too concerned about my spiritual image to ask a trusted sister in Christ to pray for me in a personal struggle with a wrong attitude or behavior?

When I find myself once again trying to apply a mask, I try to hang onto the truth that because of what Jesus did for me on the cross, God loves me just as I am. He purposely put me together in a particular way. He knows I sometimes struggle, but He also sees me as totally pure and victorious in Jesus. When I remember this, I am free to take off the makeup of false pretense and risk uncovering flaws. I'm able to wear the lip liner of truth and expose honest feelings and vulnerabilities.

To my great surprise, I have discovered that when I let go of the burden of trying to be someone I am not, I find others just as eager to drop the weight of phoniness. When I am transparent, my sisters in Christ have the freedom to do the same. In releasing the need to cover up all my flaws, I have experienced more acceptance than judgment.

Now when someone asks "How are you?" think before you answer. The standard "I'm fine" will still be required in many situations, but I hope that you will find people in your life with whom you can share your struggles and doubts. Embrace transparency and experience the freedom of life without cover-ups.

Spirit of Truth, forgive me when I have tried to be some-one I'm not. Thank You for loving me just as I am. Help me to take off the makeup of pretense and live authentically with Your people. In Jesus' name. Amen.

STEP 4

DAY 3

Lipstick Lesson

1. What is your reaction to the statement: "Authenticity scares us. So we tend to dab on a mask like we apply our makeup"?

2. Look up the word *honest,* and write several synonyms:

    a.

    b.

    c.

    d.

    How can these qualities help a relationship?

3. What principles of authenticity can you learn from these verses?
    a. Proverbs 16:13
    b. Proverbs 24:26
    c. 1 Thessalonians 2:4–6

4. What key lesson did you learn today?

5. Write out this week's memory verse. Try not to peek.

Meaningful Makeover

Reread the questions on page 101 under "Assessing Your Authenticity." Journal your responses to these questions. Write a prayer asking God to help you to live transparently. Ask Him for a few close friends with whom you can open your heart.

Speaking the Truth

Speaking the truth in love. Ephesians 4:15

Click. The phone line went dead. Silence.

What should I do? Should I try to call the person back? I didn't want to. I knew the line had not been silenced by a mechanical problem, but by the angry person on the other end.

I had picked up the ringing phone thirty minutes earlier and had been listening to a laundry list of my failures since. The last thing I wanted to do was to dial the caller's number and restart the tirade against me.

But God was nudging me to try to mend the relationship. He gave me the strength to punch in the numbers and the right words to say that eventually untangled the knots of a complicated exchange.

What bothered me about the whole conversation was not that what the caller said was untrue. In fact, I agreed with some of her points and apologized. What upset me and raised my defenses was her accusatory tone. The truth was not spoken in love.

Paul told the Ephesians:

> Speaking the truth in love, we are to grow up in every way
> into Him who is the head, into Christ, from whom the whole
> body, joined and held together by every joint with which it
> is equipped, when each part is working properly, makes the
> body grow so that it builds itself up in love.
> (Ephesians 4:15–16)

So what does speaking the truth in love mean? One thing I don't think it means is bringing every thought of mine into the open:

"Alexa, what did your stylist do to your hair? Whatever she did, she shouldn't have!"

"Been eating too many snickerdoodles lately, Lizzie? Looks like you're packing on a few extra pounds."

"Roxanne, I hate to tell you this, but that color makes you look like death warmed over. Now, don't get mad, I'm only speaking the truth in love!"

That is not speaking the truth in love. In fact, it may not even be the truth, only an opinion.

Honesty in Uncomfortable Situations

What do you do when someone asks your opinion of her outfit, work, or speech, and your honest opinion is anything but positive? Here are some suggestions for honesty in uncomfortable situations:

- Praise something specific. If you think your friend's outfit is ill-fitting, but she's wearing a fantastic necklace, make that the focus of your comment.

- Try offering a criticism between two compliments. Praise the layout and graphics of a co-worker's presentation when you need to critique the content.

- Ask permission. Ask the person if you can be perfectly honest, then offer your critique in a kind way.

- Offer your opinion as opinion. Gently give your assessment, but admit it is simply your opinion.

In examining Paul's words to the Ephesians, I see a couple of criteria about when to speak the truth in love. First, he tells us that we are to grow up into Christ. Because we are to mature spiritually, one time when we should speak the truth to brothers or sisters in Christ is when their behavior is inhibiting their relationship with God. If a friend is consistently disobeying God's instructions, we may be the person God uses to bring her back to His side.

Another time we need to speak the truth in love is when their actions are hurting the Body of Christ. Paul tells us that each part of this Body is to work together with the other parts, strengthening the whole and improving the unity. If one member is tearing down the Body instead of building it up, she may need to be confronted.

However, even if one of these two criteria is met, please pray before speaking. God may have someone else in mind to deliver the message. Or He may speak directly to the person's heart through His Word.

A Word of Truth for Today

Christ's love for me is full of patience, kindness, humility, and forgiveness.

Knowing when to speak is one part of speaking the truth in love, the other element is knowing how. I can't think of a better textbook for instruction on speaking in love than 1 Corinthians 13:

> Love is patient, love is kind. It does not envy, it does not boast, it is not proud. It is not rude, it is not self-seeking, it is not easily angered, it keeps no record of wrongs. Love does not delight in evil but rejoices with the truth. It always protects, always trusts, always hopes, always perseveres. (1 Corinthians 13:4–7 NIV)

"Love is patient, love is kind." Speaking the truth in love means speaking kindly and patiently without screaming or yelling, without cracking jokes or criticizing.

"It does not envy, it does not boast, it is not proud." Love does not have an I'm-so-glad-I-don't-have-this-problem attitude. It does mean humility and admitting your own weaknesses, especially if you have struggled with the same or a similar issue.

"It is not rude, it is not self-seeking." This is not about you. If you are speaking to make yourself feel better, that is a clue not to speak at all.

"It is not easily angered, it keeps no record of wrongs." Wait to speak until you can do it without losing your temper. Remind the person that we have all messed up in one way or another, but Jesus forgives and does not keep a running tally of the number of times we have failed.

"Love does not delight in evil but rejoices with the truth." Speaking the truth in love will not be easy or pleasant—in fact, if it brings you pleasure to point out someone's failings, you are doing it for the wrong reasons.

✝ *Even if we know when and how to speak the truth in love, our words may not be accepted. Speaking God's truth may mean disagreeing with another person's choices or lifestyle. You might be the first person to honestly confront her and she may be unwilling to change. Even if you feel that God is asking you to speak His truth, do not expect the person to receive that truth gladly.*

"It always protects, always trusts, always hopes, always perseveres." Speaking the truth in love means protecting a person's dignity. Love does not speak in a condescending tone or embarrass someone in front of a group of people. It perseveres—continuing to pray for the person after the discussion and keeping in friendly contact with him or her, if possible.

Speaking the truth in love is an important task and one that should never be taken lightly. We may not be given this assignment often, but when we are, let us be prepared to carry it out knowledgeably, kindly, respectfully, and most of all, prayerfully.

Loving Father, speaking the truth is sometimes hard. Give me guidance in the incidents when You would have me confront someone who is drifting away from You or hurting Your Church. Help me to never speak out of pride or anger, but in kindness and patience. In Jesus' name. Amen.

DAY 4

Lipstick Lesson

1. Think of when you have been on the receiving end of confrontation. Was it done with love or without? What was your reaction?

2. Which do you find more difficult: knowing when to speak the truth in love or knowing how? Why?

3. Matthew 18:15–17 gives some guidelines on confronting a believer who has sinned.

   a. Outline the steps listed.

   b. How can following these steps help to speak the truth in love?

   c. In verse 17, we see that even if everything is done correctly, the person confronted may not listen. Why do you think someone might refuse to respond to the truth?

4. What key lesson did you learn today?

5. Write out this week's memory verse. No peeking!

Meaningful Makeover

Today's lesson contained many principles on speaking the truth in love. Here or in your journal, write three or four that you especially want to remember. These insights may be useful in a current situation or sometime in the future. Writing them down will help you to recall them when you need them.

Truth in the Heart

You hypocrites! Well did Isaiah prophesy of you, when he said:
"'This people honors Me with their lips, but their heart is far
from Me". Matthew 15:7–8

It had been a busy day. Scads of people had come to Jesus from this region of Galilee when His boat had landed at Gennesaret. They brought all their sick friends and relatives, begging Jesus to heal them. Jesus performed miracle after miracle. People so sick they could not even sit up suddenly stood and walked away.

Finally, the crowd began to thin, and Jesus and the disciples sat down to eat. But just as they were taking their first bites, they noticed some men walking toward them. The men turned out to be Pharisees, who had come all the way from Jerusalem to speak to Jesus. They pulled Him aside, but kept their eyes on His friends. "Why don't Your disciples wash their hands before they eat?" they asked. "Don't they know how important it is to follow the rituals of the elders?"

Instead of answering them directly, Jesus communicated a lesson. To the Pharisees, He said, "I know you are committed to your traditions. But why are you so attached to them that you even break God's commands? God said, 'Honor your father and mother.' Yet you maintain that if a man has devoted his money to God, he doesn't have to use any of it to help his parents. You are counterfeits—pretending to honor God with your mouth even while your hearts are far away from Him."

Jesus then called the disciples and the crowd to come closer. He answered the Pharisees' original question by addressing the crowd. "Listen up, this is important. What goes into a man's mouth does not corrupt him. It's actually what comes out of his mouth that defiles him."

The disciples looked at one another. Did Jesus realize what He had done? They hurried closer to Jesus and whispered, "The Pharisees, um . . . they were . . . um . . . did You know You offended them?"

"Just ignore them," Jesus replied.

Peter spoke up, "Jesus, I'm still a little confused by what You said about what goes into a man's mouth and what comes out."

"Oh, Peter, don't you understand? Whatever goes into the mouth goes through the stomach and out again. It doesn't enter a man's soul. But what comes out of a man's mouth comes from his heart. These are the things that can pollute a person. Eating with unwashed hands doesn't defile you. The heart is the origin of the things that corrupt: evil thoughts, murder, false testimony, and slander."

Can't you feel Jesus' frustration with the Pharisees? He knew these uber-religious men were concerned about following the Law. But He also saw that they were all about outward appearance and not about inward truth. Jesus' own words to these religious leaders can teach us about truth.

Did you notice? Jesus was not afraid to speak the truth even when doing so ensured He would lose any popularity contest. The disciples were concerned about offending the Pharisees—after all, these were important people! But Jesus spoke plainly to these men who were steering others away from following God's Law.

I ask myself, "Am I more concerned with being liked than with speaking truth?" Do I sit silently when I'm at a banquet and a respected person at my table expresses a view that goes against the Bible? Am I brave enough to speak up in a meeting when someone tells an off-color joke? Jesus did not allow popularity to influence His mission of speaking the truth.

✝ *Hypocrisy is a terrible sign of trouble in our hearts— it waits only for the day of exposure. Joseph Bayly*[16]

The exchange between Jesus and the Pharisees shows how much Jesus valued truth. He called the Pharisees on their hypocrisy. Because He could see their hearts, He knew they were only play-acting. People around them were impressed, but Jesus saw behind the masks. He knew their hearts were miles away from God.

Do my words match what is in my heart? Is my voice an echo of a spirit dedicated to God? Or is it only lip-synching praise from a distracted soul? Truth is what is behind the mask. I pray my heart stays connected to my Savior and that my words will reflect that truth.

At times, I can be like one of the Pharisees—an expert at speaking just the right words. I can offer pious-sounding prayers at Bible study and sing worshipful lyrics at church. I can offer encouraging words to a friend after the service and sweetly praise a colleague. But what is really in my heart will come out of my mouth when I think no one is looking.

✝ *What comes out of my mouth when there is no one to impress is a true barometer of what is inside my heart.*

What comes out of my mouth when I'm behind closed doors and there is no one to impress? Do I yell at my kids? belittle my husband? gripe about my day? These words act as the barometer of my soul. When I hear words that would displease Jesus come out of my mouth, I know it is time to go to Him for a heart-cleaning and mouth-makeover.

A Word of Truth for Today

Jesus sees the real me behind any mask I wear, and He loves me anyway.

Truth begins in the heart. May we look honestly at all of our words, public and private, to examine what is deep inside. Allow Jesus to cleanse away any hatred, anger, or judgmental attitudes. Let's make it our aim to speak the truth to others even when that truth might be unpopular. Permit Jesus to take away any masks. May not only our lips honor Jesus, but our hearts as well.

> *Loving Savior, God of grace and truth, forgive me when I have only played the part of a Christ follower. I'm sorry for the times my words in public have made me look spiritual, but my private conversations have shown a different side of my heart. May my heart always be open to Your truth and my words reflect Your grace. In Your name. Amen.*

DAY 5

1. Write your reaction to the statement: What comes out of my mouth when there is no one to impress is a true barometer of what is inside my heart.

2. Read Matthew 15:1–20.

   a. Look up the word *hypocrite* in the dictionary and write the definition:

   b. Why did Jesus call the Pharisees hypocrites?

   c. At times, we all probably honor God with our lips while our hearts are far from Him. How can we bring our words and our hearts into alignment?

3. LIP Study

This week, we will study Proverbs 26:18–28 (NIV) using the three-step LIP process to uncover principles of honest speech. Because verses in Proverbs are already stated in principles, try using modern analogies when you interpret the meaning. Read through the passage three times and follow these steps (I have done a few for you as examples):

Look for the Facts

Interpret the Meaning

Pursue the Application

Look for the facts. Don't make any interpretations here. Simply write what is happening in each verse.

Verses 18–19 A madman shooting arrows is like a man who lies to his neighbor.

Verse 20   Gossip dies down if no one repeats it.

Verse 21

Verse 22

Verse 23

Verse 24

Verse 25

Verse 26

Verse 27

Verse 28

Interpret the meaning. Turn the lesson in the passage into a scriptural principle. (This week, you might try your hand at making a modern proverb.)

Verses 18–19 Lying and then joking about it is as dangerous as a drive-by shooting.

Verse 20 Put the lid on a candle and watch the flame go out; put your hand over your mouth and watch the gossip die down.

Verse 21

Verse 22

Verse 23

Verse 24

Verse 25

Verse 26

Verse 27

Verse 28

Pursue the application. Turn the principle you discovered into a personal question that applies the truth to your life.

Verses 18–19 Do I realize the dire consequences of lying? Or do I only perceive it as a joke?

Verse 20 Do I contribute to the spread of gossip? Or do I stop it in its tracks?

Verse 21

Verse 22

Verse 23

Verse 24

Verse 25

Verse 26

Verse 27

Verse 28

4. What key lesson did you learn today?

STEP 4

5. Write Psalm 34:12–13 (NIV) from memory.

Meaningful Makeover

Choose one question from those you posed in "Pursue the Application." Answer it honestly and come up with an action you can do to grow in that area.

Color:
Choose Words with Grace

Memory Verse

Let your speech always be gracious, seasoned with salt, so that you may know how you ought to answer each person.
Colossians 4:6

DAY 1

Full of Grace

Let your speech always be gracious, seasoned with salt, so that
you may know how you ought to answer each person.
Colossians 4:6

Sensitive hearts. Open Bibles. Honest conversation. These are the ingredients for a great Bible study group. Add some good coffee and a little laughter and it becomes a recipe you want to repeat over and over again.

Not long ago, I met with a group of young moms that had all of those ingredients. We sat around a kitchen table sharing egg casserole, fruit salad, and what God was doing in our lives. Although I had just met these ladies, I could tell they were women of deep faith.

This women shared openly about their struggles with their children. They confessed that they felt they were yelling all the time. Although they didn't want to, they found themselves raising their voices and shouting things like:

"Hurry up! We have to be at school in five minutes!"

"Don't you have your shoes on yet?"

"How many times do I have to tell you? It's time to go to bed!"

I also admitted that although I am usually soft-spoken, I often found myself yelling at my children when they were young. I confessed I was sometimes shocked at the tone that came out of my mouth. And I told these young mothers that I had discovered my propensity to yell increased whenever I was tired.

Almost in unison, they said, "Then I must be tired all the time!"

These mothers were honest about their battles in choosing the right words for their children. And, of course, most of us struggle with this. We want to choose words that build up our families and improve our friendships, but we are not always successful.

Choosing the right shade of lipstick can be challenging as well. When I visited a makeup expert for a Mouth Makeover, she exfoliated my lips, soothed them with lip balm, plumped them up a bit, and applied lip liner. Next, she smoothed on rich color. I was astounded that she instantly chose the perfect shade to enhance my smile. I can't tell you how many tubes of lipstick I have purchased that looked like a flattering shade in the package, but ended up looking like pink cotton candy or blood-red catsup on my lips. However, the makeup expert lived up to her title and knew the exact shade I needed.

How to Pick a Perfect Shade of Lipstick

- Choose a shade one or two shades darker than your bare lip color.
- If you have cool undertones in your skin, wear cool reds and pinks.
- If you have warm undertones, pick peach and coral shades.

The apostle Paul also tells us the exact shade of speech that we need. He advises us in Colossians 4:6, "Let your speech always be gracious." Grace is the color that is always appropriate. Gracious speech is exactly what our family and friends need.

What exactly is grace? Grace is one of those churchy words that we often use, but may not actually understand. This week, we will explore several meanings of the Greek word translated as grace—*charis*. Understanding the term will help us develop more gracious speech. Look at the first definition of charis: "that which affords joy, pleasure, delight, sweetness, charm, loveliness, grace of speech."[17] According to this definition, the color of speech that will always be appropriate is sweet, charming, and graceful. How can we learn to leave the shades of Insensitive Iris and Rude Red in their tubes and instead consistently choose to wear shades of grace?

Shades of Grace

- Courteous Coral: Remember to say "please" and "thank you."
- Listening Lilac: Establish eye contact, and don't interrupt.
- Respectful Ruby: Treat others as you would like to be treated.
- Inclusive Iris: Help others to feel a part of the group.
- Contrite Carmine: Apologize when you've made a mistake.

One way I try to do this is to simply remember my manners. In our hurry-up world, it is easy to forget common courtesies. My family has always tried to remember to use those magic words of "please" and "thank you." Using courtesy even when it's "just family" is one way to choose the shade of grace.

Respect is also an important ingredient in speaking with grace. I experience joy and pleasure when talking with someone who listens attentively, maintains eye contact, and asks thoughtful questions at appropriate times. But I have also been annoyed when the person I am conversing with interrupts me, answers every cell phone call, dismisses my opinions, or is clearly bored or distracted. Remembering to treat the other person as you would want to be treated is another way to consistently speak with grace.

Selecting shades of grace also means rejecting terrifying tones of voice. Although I may not currently have a problem of yelling (I usually get enough sleep now that my children are grown), speaking through clenched teeth does not demonstrate grace either. How about whining impatience or biting sarcasm? I pray that the sound of my voice will demonstrate grace.

The young mothers in the Bible study group I visited truly wanted gracious speech. While they were talking about their struggles, I remembered a young mother, named Jenny, who wrote a comment on my blog. I shared her comment as a beautiful way to offer gracious speech to their children. Jenny wrote:

> EVERY night I hold each child close, look eye to eye and say,
> "You are a beautiful, wonderful child of God, and Mom and
> Dad love you always and forever no matter what." They line
> up waiting for their turn each night and soak it up.

After I told the group her words, I looked down and sheepishly said, "I wish I would have thought of doing that when my kids were young."

When I looked up, all the eyes around the table were brimming with tears.

A Word of Grace for Today

You are a beautiful, wonderful child of God, and the Father loves you always and forever, no matter what.

Gracious Father, I confess that my conversations are not always filled with grace. I'm frustrated with myself when disrespectful words roll off my tongue and when the tone of my voice is grating to the soul. Father, help me to speak words that bless others. Enable me to speak grace to the people You place in my path today. In Jesus' name. Amen.

DAY 1

Lipstick Lesson

1. What is your favorite shade of lipstick? If you are in a group, bring it along to the meeting. Tell why it is your favorite color.

2. Reread the "Shades of Grace" sidebar on page 117.

    a. When others speak to you, which shade do you most appreciate?

    b. Which shade do you need to work on in your own speech?

3. The Bible often describes our speech in word pictures that demonstrate helpful and hurtful words. For the following verses, write the descriptive terms used and some examples that fit that description.

STEP 5

	Descriptive terms used	Examples of speech
a. Psalm 59:7	Example: swords from their lips	Example: angry words
b. Psalm 64:3		
c. Proverbs 16:24		
d. Proverbs 20:15		

Which word picture will you keep in mind today to remind yourself to speak graciously?

4. What key lesson did you learn today?

5. Write out our memory verse for this week: "Let your speech always be gracious, seasoned with salt, so that you may know how you ought to answer each person" (Colossians 4:6). To help you memorize this passage, write it out in the space below. You might also put on some lipstick and practice saying this verse in front of a mirror.

Meaningful Makeover

Today concentrate on speaking words of grace. Perhaps you will focus on the Shade of Grace you picked in Question 2b. Journal here about what speaking grace looks like in your life.

The Color of Contention

The Lord's servant must not be quarrelsome. 2 Timothy 2:24a

I will never forget Elijah. He was a first grader at the neighborhood public school where I was volunteering. Although most of the students I was working with were eager to learn, Elijah was a troublemaker. Standing in line to go to recess, he would shove the person in front of him just enough to be annoying. When the students were supposed to be working at their desks, Elijah would get up and stand very close to another student and stare long enough to make him uncomfortable. If he was bored, he might grab someone else's pencil and claim it as his own as the other person protested.

Elijah loved to pick a fight. He was quarrelsome.

Unfortunately, I have also known some adults like Elijah. Adults who still love to pick a fight. For instance, I know one woman who regularly takes offense over minor disagreements, and if she feels she has been wronged, she refuses to speak to the offender for years. Another acquaintance attends workshops merely to disagree with the presenter, annoying everyone who has come to learn.

Instead of wearing shades of grace and speaking words that bring joy and pleasure, these people wear the colors of dissension, controversy, and irritation.

What does the Bible say about those who love to argue?

> Have nothing to do with foolish, ignorant controversies;
> you know that they breed quarrels. And the Lord's servant
> must not be quarrelsome but kind to everyone, able to
> teach, patiently enduring evil, correcting his opponents with
> gentleness. (2 Timothy 2:23–25a)

In this passage, Paul is speaking to Timothy. He tells him to stay away from controversy. And he instructs us all as servants of the Lord to avoid quarrels.

Why are quarreling and squabbling popular sports for some people? Perhaps they were raised in a home with a nightly debate around the dinner table, every meal a match of reason and wit.

Others may participate in the sport of disputing because that is how they prop up their self-worth. They make themselves feel important by attacking another's ideas and beliefs. Author Deborah Smith Pegues observes:

> The quarreler's goal is not to add value to someone's life by showing him the error of his way. In fact, Mrs. Quarreler would be greatly disappointed if her target responded, "Oh, thank you for shedding light on this matter. I will change my thinking immediately." Why, such a concession would end the argument![18]

Still others may not instigate an argument, but if someone questions their opinions, they rise to the challenge. They are ready to defend their views and prove their position no matter what cost to the relationship with the other person.

Quieting Quarrelers

Some steps to take when you find yourself in a discussion that's escalating into an argument:

- Stay calm. Even if the other person is raising his voice, don't yell back.

- Change the subject. Ask the other person about another less emotional topic.

- Ask permission to share your view. Even someone who loves to argue will have to listen to your side if she consents.

- Give some thought to the other person's opinion. Point out any points of agreement and then explain where you differ.

- Agree to disagree. When it is apparent that you will never see eye to eye, tell the other person that you respect him but, on this matter, you can't share his opinion.

What does Paul tell us to do instead? He instructs us to treat everyone with kindness and patience even if it means we have to put up with some nasty remarks. He encourages us to correct with gentleness instead of arrogance.

Sometimes, it's easy to participate in an argument if the issue is something we feel strongly about, like a religious belief or a political stand. But we need to remember that arguments rarely transform opinions. Treating someone with respect and consideration may do more to change a person's mind than the best-worded defense. Quietly stating our views may be more convincing than any heated discussion.

> ✞ *People's minds are changed through observation and*
> *not through argument. Will Rogers*[19]

Perhaps, the biggest challenge is when we know our beliefs are supported by the Bible, but the person holding an opposing belief refuses to listen. Then we must leave it to God. Paul continued teaching Timothy, "God may perhaps grant them repentance leading to a knowledge of the truth" (2 Timothy 2:25b). Only God can truly change hearts.

The God of peace urges us not to wear shades of speech in the colors of dissension and disagreement. Let minor matters slide; we don't have to defend every opinion. And where we find ourselves discussing faith and values, we can gently state our views, defer to a higher authority (our pastor!), and, perhaps, agree to disagree.

> ✞ *The Holy Spirit is the magnificent Heart Changer.*
> *He alone is able to lead people to a knowledge of the truth.*

Honor God by your gentle and respectful speech. Win others over with love instead of argument. Wear shades of grace instead of the color of contention.

> *God of peace, teach me to be Your true servant, reach-*
> *ing others with kindness instead of disputes. Give me wis-*
> *dom to know when to drop a matter and when to defend my*
> *view with grace. Help me to always remember that love is*
> *more persuasive than any argument. In Jesus' name. Amen.*

DAY 2

Lipstick Lesson

STEP 5

1. Do you like to wear the color of contention or do you avoid it at all costs? Talk about your preference and the reason behind it.

2. God's Word gives insight into quieting a quarrel. What can you learn from these passages?
    a. Proverbs 17:14
    b. Judges 8:1–3

3. What do these verses tell us about quarrelers?
    a. Proverbs 17:19
    b. Proverbs 20:3
    c. How do these passages motivate you to avoid quarreling?

4. What key lesson did you learn today?

5. Write out our memory verse for this week: "Let your speech always be gracious, seasoned with salt, so that you may know how you ought to answer each person" (Colossians 4:6). Read a phrase, then cover it and write it. Recite as much of the verse as you can without looking.

Meaningful Makeover

In the space here or in your journal, write a prayer asking God to help you avoid quarrelling and contention. Address any potential situations at home or at work that may trigger heated discussions. Call on God to give you wisdom and patience in those times.

A Constant Dripping

A continual dripping on a rainy day and a quarrelsome wife are alike; to restrain her is to restrain the wind or to grasp oil in one's right hand. Proverbs 27:15–16

Rain battered the windows of my family room. The sound of the pelting rain nearly drowned out the television. I was sitting in my usual spot on the sofa, trying to watch a favorite show, but I wondered, *Will it happen again?*

It did.

A drop of water fell from the ceiling and landed in my lap. Another drop and another followed. I got up, walked over to the windows, and rolled up the shade. Water was also dripping from the windows *inside* the house.

We were having trouble with the roof above our family room. Every time we had a downpour, we had to put towels in the windows and a bucket on the couch where I usually sat. From the outside of the house, you couldn't see any problem with the roof. But whenever it rained, it was obvious from the inside that there was trouble.

This can also be true with my mouth. If you met me at a coffee shop and we chatted for awhile, you might never suspect I had an unruly mouth. But if you put a hidden camera in my house, it probably wouldn't take too long before you heard the drip, drip of a woman with a mouth problem.

Is that true for you too? We often hurt those we love the most and our weapon of choice is our words. We don't set out to be hurtful. I don't imagine any of us said "I do" to our husbands with the thought, "Oh, good—now I have someone to hassle about eating habits. Finally, I can give constant reminders about household chores!" When we envisioned starting a family, we didn't do so because we wanted to continually shout orders to pick up clothes and put away toys.

From the outside, no one might suspect a speech problem. But inside the house, there is a constant dripping. Within the walls, there might be signs of what the Book of Proverbs calls "a quarrelsome wife." Don't like that term? Other versions translate the words as: "a woman full of chiding," "a contentious woman," and "a nagging spouse."

I know. Those terms are no better, but sometimes they are true. Why does our speech sometimes degenerate to this point? Why does my mouth seem to automatically spew out orders or churn out nagging statements when I really want my home to be a haven?

One motive we may have for wearing the shade of Nagging Nectarine is concern for the people in our lives. We want them to be healthy so we say, "Eat your broccoli" or ask, "You're having *another* cookie?" We want them to be successful so we prod, "Finish your homework" or "Update your résumé."

But there may be another explanation for our use of nagging words: We want to be in control. Because we want the house to look a particular way, we are apt to say things like: "Pick up your socks already!" "When are you going to get around to painting the trim on the house?" We say that we love the people in our lives, yet we want to fix what's wrong with them, so we spout: "Straighten up your posture." "Speak up for yourself at work!"

No-Nag Zone: Dos and Don'ts for Dealing with Adults

You don't want to be a nag, but sometimes the people in your life need a little "reminding." Here are some guidelines for building a No-Nag Zone in your home or office:

Don't

- Don't demean or attack. Talk about the issue.
- Don't use phrases like "You always—" or "You never—."
- Don't use a condescending or commanding tone of voice.

Do

- Do notice the other person's efforts. Express appreciation!
- Do use common courtesy—say "please" and "thank you."
- Do remember nagging doesn't work.

When you hear yourself nagging, ask yourself why. Be honest. Are you simply trying to offer advice out of concern? Or are your words based in control issues? Are you trying to change your husband, your child, your friend?

When I recognize my tendency to control, I ask God to change me. He is, after all, the One who is truly in charge. He knows what the other person needs more than I do. Sometimes, it is my place to help another person to change, but often, my role is simply to pray for God's will in their lives.

And if constant reminders tumble out of my mouth out of love for my family members or friends, I need to remember that it doesn't feel like love to them. Continual prompting feels like distrust and disapproval. A steady stream of instruction and advice can give the impression that my affection has to be earned by jumping through specific hoops.

A Word of Grace for Today

God does not withhold His love for me until I have reached a certain standard. He loves me unconditionally.

No matter what motivates me to recite a repertoire of reminders, I need to remember the apostle Paul's advice, "Let your speech always be gracious" (Colossians 4:6). The first definition of grace taught us that graceful speech gives joy and pleasure. A home full of chiding and nagging will not be an atmosphere of joy. A workplace full of contention will never bring pleasure.

No-Nag Zone: Suggestions for Dealing with Kids

Here are a few practical suggestions for building a No-Nag Zone in your home by reducing the need for reminders:

• Establish routines. Build in the habits of hanging up backpacks after school, putting dirty plates in the sink after dinner.

• Try chore charts. Kids usually love to keep track of what they've done on a chart. It's amazing what they will do for a sticker or small prize!

• Give a heads up. Warning your kids—"Ten minutes until bedtime" or "Supper will be ready in five minutes"—gives them time to shift gears.

• Be consistent and firm. Expect your children to obey the first time. Enforcing consequences when they don't will eliminate the need to repeat yourself.

• Praise your child's efforts!

Perhaps a key element in choosing speech in the shades of grace is found in the second definition of *charis:* "good will, loving-kindness, favor—the merciful kindness by which God turns people to Christ."[20] Although I am far from perfect, my heavenly Father offers me loving-kindness. Yes, God often has to show me where I have strayed from His path, but He is patient with me. He doesn't withhold His affection until I have reached a particular point of progress in my spiritual growth. If I keep this in mind, perhaps I can offer the same kind of grace to the people in my life. Perhaps I will be more likely to extend mercy instead of disapproval if I fully appreciate God's gift of loving-kindness.

The next time nagging words threaten to tumble out of your mouth, examine your motivation. Ask God to work the change needed in the other person and in your attitude. Accept the gift of the Father's loving-kindness and offer it to others. Instead of the drip, drip, drip of nagging and contention, let's fill our homes and workplaces with a flood of grace.

Loving Lord, I praise You for Your mercy. Thank You for loving me even though I have such a long way to go in my spiritual journey. Forgive me when I have not exhibited the same patience with the people around me. I truly desire to create an atmosphere of joy and acceptance in my home. Enable me to speak in shades of grace. In Jesus' name. Amen.

DAY 3

Lipstick Lesson

1. What is your definition of nagging?

2. Recall a time when you felt nagged by a parent, spouse, or friend. What were your emotions? How did you perceive the other person's intentions?

3. What does the Book of Proverbs have to say about a quarrelsome wife? (Obviously, the same things could be said about a quarrelsome husband.)

   a. Proverbs 19:13

   b. Proverbs 21:9

   c. Proverbs 21:19

   d. Name a few steps you can take when you are tempted to become a quarrelsome or nagging woman. (You might choose some of the suggestions from today's lesson.)

4. What key lesson did you learn today?

5. Write out this week's memory verse. Try not to peek!

Meaningful Makeover

Take some time today to thank God for His grace, mercy, and patience. Write a prayer of gratitude below. Keep this prayer in mind as you go through your day. Journal about how focusing on God's grace changed the words you spoke to the people in your life.

DAY 4

Sharing God's Grace

STEP 5

And I, when I came to you, brothers, did not come proclaiming
to you the testimony of God with lofty speech or wisdom.
1 Corinthians 2:1

My friend Sue is an evangelist. She doesn't call herself that since she doesn't travel to distant countries as a missionary or ring doorbells in other towns. Sue, in fact, works at an accountant's office. Her job description does not include reciting Bible verses or passing out tracts. Nevertheless, Sue shares what Jesus means to her whenever she gets the chance. Among cubicles and computers, she lives out her faith and the people in her office take notice. Because she demonstrates patience and peace, her co-workers come to her for advice and prayer. In the chaos of tax season, they ask Sue how she can stay so calm and she tells them, "It's because I have Jesus in my life and He makes all the difference."

A Word of Grace for Today

Jesus renews my life, changes my perspective, and improves the path I'm on. He makes all the difference.

I wish I was more like Sue. The truth is that I do not personally share my faith very often. Yes, when I'm speaking to women's groups, I frequently share my faith story and talk about the difference Jesus makes in my life. But in daily conversation, I often shy away from the topic of faith.

Why am I comfortable sharing my faith in one setting and not the other? One reason for my reluctance to talk about Jesus in a personal conversation is fear of rejection. When I'm speaking to a group, it is expected that I share my faith. But mention Jesus to someone after a business meeting? They might think I'm weird.

I also hesitate to share my faith in a personal way for fear of getting tongue-tied and saying the wrong thing. My public speeches are carefully written and rehearsed, but I don't have a speech manuscript to fall back on when I'm in a conversation with a friend.

Practical Steps to Sharing Your Faith

- Pray for people in your life who don't know Jesus.
- Ask God to make you aware of people who are hurting or searching.
- Look for opportunities to share encouragement, hope, and the Gospel.
- Be ready to tell about your relationship with Jesus.

Still, speaking about Jesus is something I want to do more often. After all, telling others about Christ is the most important thing we can do with our mouths. Sharing God's grace is a high privilege.

Maybe you, too, find it difficult to talk comfortably about your faith. Let's look at the apostle Paul's words to the people of Corinth to gain instruction and inspiration:

> And I, when I came to you, brothers, did not come proclaiming to you the testimony of God with lofty speech or wisdom. For I decided to know nothing among you except Jesus Christ and Him crucified. And I was with you in weakness and in fear and much trembling, and my speech and my message were not in plausible words of wisdom, but in demonstration of the Spirit and of power, so that your faith might not rest in the wisdom of men but in the power of God. (1 Corinthians 2:1–5)

First of all, I notice that Paul says, "when I came to you." He didn't wait for non-Christians to come to him. Sometimes, the first step to leading people to Jesus is to go to them. I'm a pastor's wife. I hang out at church and at Bible study. Most of the people I know are Christian. So one thing I have chosen to do is join a few secular organizations to make new friends who may not have a relationship with Jesus yet.

Paul also told the Corinthians that he did not come with "lofty speech or wisdom." Paul tells us that he didn't use eloquent speech. Although he was a renowned speaker, he knew that big words don't speak to people's hearts. We may be afraid of stumbling over our words, but it is helpful to remember that honest communication will be more convincing than any rehearsed speech.

I was surprised to see that the highly-educated Paul experienced "fear and much trembling" like I sometimes do. But it turns out that any weakness I may feel may be an advantage because then I will be more likely to rely on the power of God. Paul told the Corinthians he didn't use big words of wisdom because he wanted them to see a "demonstration of the Spirit and of power." Self-confidence may enable me to give an articulate speech, but reliance on the Spirit will give me words that penetrate the soul. And no matter what words I use, I need to remember that it is only the Holy Spirit that truly changes hearts.

Questions to Start a Conversation about Jesus

- What is your spiritual background?
- Does faith play a role in your perspective on life?
- Do you think Christianity is still relevant today?
- What do you believe about God?
- Do you mind if I share my views about Jesus?

"I decided to know nothing among you except Jesus Christ and Him crucified" (1 Corinthians 2:2). Maybe this will help most of all: to concentrate on the message of Jesus. Witnessing is not simply sharing a plan of salvation. It is introducing a Friend. It is leading someone into a relationship with the almighty God.

So let's talk about Jesus. Paint a picture of the Man who took time to hold children in His arms. Convey the truth of the Son of God who was willing to come to earth and be beaten up because He loved us. Talk about the One who was willing to die a horrifying death so we could have a relationship with Him. Tell about the God who defeated death so we no longer have to fear it.

May our conversations always be full of grace. May we be willing to tell others about God's mercy and loving kindness. May we speak up and say, "I have Jesus in my life and He makes all the difference."

My loving Savior, I confess that I am often hesitant to speak about my relationship with You. I am ashamed to say it. But, Lord, I want to change that. Help me to notice people around me who need You. Give me the right words to tell them about You, my best Friend. In Your name. Amen.

DAY 4

Lipstick Lesson

1. What emotions do you feel when you hear the phrase "share your faith"?

2. Reread the sidebar "Questions to Start a Conversation about Jesus" (p. 132). Which questions would you be comfortable using?

3. The woman at the well is often said to be the first female evangelist. Although you may have heard it many times, try to read the story in John 4:1–45 with fresh eyes.

   a. Based on verses 16–17, which of the following statements do you most agree with?

      • Jesus must have chosen this woman to be a witness because she was so good.

      • The woman had a less-than-pristine character.

      • Any mission board would be glad to have her as their representative.

   b. Look at verses 28–29. Which of the following statements do you most agree with?

      • The woman told her story in big theological terms.

      • The woman told what she did for Jesus.

      • The woman told of her personal experience with Jesus.

   c. Based on verses 28–30, which statement below do you most agree with?

      • The woman dropped everything and told the people in her town she had met the Messiah.

      • After meeting Jesus, the woman went right back to her business and didn't tell anyone about Him.

      • The woman avoided the people in her town, and instead traveled to the next county to tell them the Good News about Jesus.

   d. Which statement in the list that follows do you most agree with, based on verses 39–42?

      • No one in the woman's town was affected by her testimony.

      • Everyone who believed did so because of her words.

• The woman's words spurred an interest in Jesus, and many more believed because of His words.

e. Summarize what you have just learned about being an evangelist.

4. What key lesson did you learn today?

5. Write out this week's memory verse. Try not to peek!

Meaningful Makeover

Take the first step to sharing your faith. Write the names of three people in your family, workplace, or circle of friends who don't know Jesus personally. Write out a prayer that their hearts would be open to a relationship with Him. Ask God to give you the right opportunity and the best words to communicate His love. Commit to praying for these people every day.

The Greatest Need of All

And when Jesus saw their faith, He said to the paralytic, "Son, your sins are forgiven." Mark 2:5

An elbow jammed into my side. Someone pushed me from behind. The stifling air in the room was beginning to make me feel light-headed. But, I thought, at least I won't fall if I faint. There are so many people crammed into this house I'd be held up by the crowd!

Still more people were peering into the open door trying to get a glimpse of the man speaking in the center of the room. This teacher had become a major topic of conversation in the past few days. People were sharing implausible reports of His ability to heal diseases and cast out demons. Many people in this room had come for their own healing. Some had come to hear His teaching. I had come to determine this scam artist's tricks.

I was watching Him closely when specks of dust and dirt began falling in front of His face. Larger chunks of debris began to fall and the people in front of me pushed backward squeezing the crowd even tighter. Suddenly, daylight filled the room and four faces appeared in a hole in the roof! One of the four faces shouted, "There He is! There's Jesus!"

Someone inside the room muttered, "What do they think they are doing? Look what they have done to poor Jacob's roof!"

The faces in the sunlit hole disappeared only to be replaced by a sleeping mat attached to some ropes. As the mat slowly descended into the room, I saw a man lying on it. He made no effort to hang onto the mat or balance himself during his shaky descent. His limbs were withered from many years of disease.

Now I would be able to discover the truth about this Jesus. Surely there was no cure for the man on the cot. I would be able to tell my friends that Jesus was a charlatan, a false teacher.

Jesus held up His hand to quiet the murmuring crowd. He turned His eyes to the man on the mat and said, "Son, your sins are forgiven."

What? Who does this guy think He is? Only God can forgive sins!

I now had the proof I needed. Not only was Jesus powerless to heal this man, He was trying to mask His inability with spiritual sounding words that amounted to blasphemy.

Jesus spoke again, "I know what you are thinking. But so you may know that the Son of Man has the authority to forgive sins." He paused and looked at the paralyzed man, "I tell you, get up, take your mat and go home."

I wouldn't have believed it if I hadn't seen it with my own eyes, but the man's seemingly dead limbs suddenly moved. He sat up, swung his legs off the mat and stood. He gathered up his mat and the cheering crowd made room for him to walk out the door on his own feet.

✟ *In the Gospel, the Good News of our salvation in Jesus Christ, God gives forgiveness, faith, life, and the power to please Him with good works.*

Picture yourself in that crowded house in Capernaum. Do you identify with the people in the crowd who were there to hear words of hope? Or would you have been one of the skeptics?

What would your reaction have been when the paralytic was lowered into the already crowded room? Would you have felt compassion toward the paralyzed man? Would you have been indignant at the men who had the gall to destroy someone's roof? Would you have wondered if this whole incident was part of some elaborate ruse?

Tell the truth; would your first impulse have been, "This man needs forgiveness"?

Jesus' immediate reaction was to offer grace. He didn't scold the friends for property damage or deliver a lecture to the paralyzed man. He even overlooked the man's more obvious physical needs and addressed the needs of his heart. Jesus' first words to the man on the mat were "Son, your sins are forgiven."

✟ *Jesus satisfies our deepest need: grace.*

This week, we have been talking about the definitions of *charis*, the Greek word translated as grace. The third meaning of charis is "what is due to grace—the spiritual condition of one governed by the power of divine grace."[21] Obviously, Jesus was always governed by the power of divine grace. He is true God as well as true man. He always determined to do the will of His Father. His life on earth is the model of a life controlled by the power of grace.

Because the Holy Spirit lives in me, I also have the opportunity to live a life dominated by an attitude of grace, yet my sinful nature often wins out with attitudes of judgment, impatience, or bitterness. I try to keep these attitudes hidden, yet my tone of voice may indicate my intolerance. My words may belie my irritation. My comments may reveal my resentment.

✝ *I desire to live a life controlled by the power of divine grace.*

Looking at Jesus' words to the man on the cot, I see that we all need grace more than anything else, whether we realize it or not. If I want to live a life governed by grace, I need to remember this fact and embrace God's love.

Let's see others with the eyes of Jesus. Look for times to give grace in simple kindnesses. Search out occasions to overlook a fault rather than give nit-picking criticism. Take advantage of opportunities to repair a relationship with mercy.

Most of all, let's lead people to the One who will speak the words, "Your sins are forgiven."

> *Merciful Savior, You see my deepest need. You know that more than anything I need Your grace. Help me to see others in the same way: humans in need of Your mercy and forgiveness. Give me the ability to convey grace through words of kindness, love, and patience. Help me to tell others of Your saving grace. In Your name. Amen.*

DAY 5

Lipstick Lesson

1. Read the story of Jesus healing the paralytic in Mark 2:1–12. Picture yourself in the crowded room in Capernaum. Where do you see yourself in the story, and what reactions might you have felt?

2. LIP Study

Our memory verse this week is Colossians 4:6. Today we will study this verse in context. Read Colossians 3:13–17 and 4:2–6 and use the three-step LIP process to uncover principles of gracious speech. Read through the passage three times and follow these steps (I have done a few for you as examples):

Look for the Facts

Interpret the Meaning

Pursue the Application

Look for the facts. Don't make any interpretations here. Simply write what is happening in each verse.

3:13 Be patient with others and forgive as God forgave you.

3:14 Put on love most of all.

3:15 Let the peace of Christ rule in your hearts

3:16

3:17

4:2

4:3

4:4

4:5

4:6

Interpret the meaning. Turn the lesson in the passage into a scriptural principle.

3:13 Because God extended grace to us, we can extend grace to others.

3:14 Love is the most important thing we can give to others.

138

3:15 The peace I have because of Christ's forgiveness should be a controlling force in my life.

3:16

3:17

4:2

4:3

4:4

4:5

4:6

Pursue the application. Turn the principle you discovered into a personal question that applies the truth to your life.

3:13 Do I fully appreciate the gift of God's grace? Do I give the same grace and forgiveness to others?

3:14 Do I usually give love to the people in my family? Or am I more likely to give criticism, reminders, and reprimands?

3:15 Am I conscious of the peace that I have in Jesus? Do I let it rule my heart?

3:16

3:17

4:2

4:3

4:4

4:5

4:6

3. What key lesson did you learn today?

4. Write Colossians 4:6 from memory.

Meaningful Makeover

Choose one question from those you posed in "Pursue the Application." Answer it honestly and come up with an action you can do to grow in that area.

STEP 6

Gloss:
Shine with Thankfulness

Memory Verse

Give thanks in all circumstances; for this is the will of God in Christ Jesus for you. 1 Thessalonians 5:18

Whining Wine

They grumbled in their tents and did not obey the LORD.
Psalm 106:25 NIV

I met Karen on the first day of grad school. Because we were working toward the same degree, we made an instant connection. Karen had attended the school the year before and filled me in on which classes to take and which professors to avoid. I felt like I was getting useful insider information. But I soon noticed that every tidbit she shared was negative. There was something wrong with every class. Every teacher was either boring or demanding. All the other students were unfairly promoted to her disadvantage.

I began to question my decision in choosing this school. That is until I discovered inspiring teachers, caring students, and interesting classes. Soon I recognized Karen for what she was—a chronic complainer. Karen was always wearing speech in the shade of Whining Wine.

✝ *Leave the shade of Whining Wine in the tube and wear the lip gloss of thankfulness instead.*

The Bible also talks about some grumblers. In fact, the Book of Numbers records the whining and muttering of a whole nation of chronic complainers. The Israelites were famous for their escape from Pharaoh and for their journey through the Red Sea, but they were not known for their positive attitude.

Only three days into their journey to the Promised Land, "the people complained in the hearing of the LORD about their misfortunes" (Numbers 11:1a). Now granted, at this point, they had been living in tents at the base of Mount Sinai for a year. Since I'm not a big fan of camping, I probably would have been one of the first to gripe about the housing arrangements. But God had saved them from the hardships of slavery and was now leading them to a new land. You would have thought they would have been excited about the prospect of life in their own country without Pharaoh telling them what to do. Instead they complained about their misfortunes! Maybe talk around the camp went something like this: "My feet are so sore from walking in this stinkin' desert!" "My back aches from pulling our cart. Did you have to bring so many shoes?" "Are we there yet?"

God was not amused by the talk. In fact, "when the LORD heard it, His anger was kindled, and the fire of the LORD burned among them and consumed some outlying parts of the camp" (Numbers 11:1b). God demonstrated His displeasure about the murmuring and muttering in a very powerful and fiery way. There could have been no doubt that God was upset.

But did that stop the Israelites from carping? No. They continued to grumble and God delivered more consequences. Miriam contracted leprosy when she and Aaron complained about Moses' Cushite wife (Numbers 12:1–10). When the Israelites whined, "Would that we had died in the land of Egypt!" (Numbers 14:2), God sentenced them to forty more years of wandering in the desert. And in a dramatic display of God's displeasure with the complaints of Korah and his clan, the earth opened beneath them and swallowed them up (Numbers 16:1–33).

God clearly hates complaining. What makes grumbling so offensive to God? I see an answer to that question in Numbers 14:11 where God says, "How long will these people despise Me?" I may hate whining because of the irritating tone of voice people use. Carping may be grating to my nerves. But when God hears complaining, He hears words of disdain and disrespect.

Conquering Constant Complaining

Not ready to give up complaining just yet? Perhaps this list of the negative effects of grumbling will motivate you.

• Complaining digs your rut deeper. Ruminating over your problems tends to amplify them.

• Grumbling focuses your attention on the negative. Walking around in a dark cloud may prevent you from seeing the good in your life.

• Negative people spread gloom in the world. Griping actually puts stress on the person to whom you are complaining.

• Constant complainers alienate themselves from other people. No one wants to be around a person who is constantly gloomy.

Think about it from God's point of view. He had just saved the Israelites from a life of slavery under a cruel Pharaoh. He had told them that He would bless them and make them His very own people. He promised them a land flowing with milk and honey. But the people complained about the food. They whined about living in the desert. They grumbled because someone else was calling all the shots. Seemingly minor stuff compared to a life of hunger and hard labor. To God's ears, all those murmurings sounded like lack of appreciation for all the miraculous things He had done for them. It sounded like contempt.

A Word of Thankfulness for Today

Thank You, Father. By sending Jesus to the cross to take the punishment for my sins, You rescued me from the slavery of sin and eternal death. Thank You for Your freeing gifts of unfailing love and everlasting salvation.

I can tsk-tsk the Israelites, but am I any different? God has given me a wonderful husband, loving children, and a beautiful home. And yet what do I complain about? The weather is lousy. I'm tired of cooking. So-and-so thinks she knows everything. Instead of a grateful heart, I display a dissatisfied attitude and, judging from the stories in the Book of Numbers, I don't think God is pleased.

Now that I realize that my grumbling insults God, I am more motivated to eliminate complaining words from my vocabulary. My soul aches at the thought that my mindless carping sounds like open disdain in God's ears. I pray that instead of spouting complaints, I will express gratitude for the gifts my heavenly Father has already given.

This week, let's recall God's words to the Israelites. And when complaining words begin to tumble out of our mouths, let's remember how our bellyaching actually hurts our Lord. Let's leave the shade of Whining Wine in the drawer and wear the gloss of thankfulness on our lips instead.

Father in heaven, I am sorry when I have grumbled and griped about my life. Too many times I have been like the Israelites—complaining about minor problems when You have given me so much. Help me to remember to say "thank You." In Jesus' name. Amen.

DAY 1

Lipstick Lesson

1. This week, we are talking about eliminating the shade of Whining Wine and instead wearing the gloss of thankfulness. How can complaining words dull your image?

2. Where do you fall on the Complaining Scale?

I usually keep my discontent a secret.   Whenever I am dissatisfied, I let everyone know.

- -

Honestly assess your complaining habits and mark an X where you fall between these two extremes.

3. Talk about the negative effects of complaining listed in the sidebar on page 142. Which have you found to be true in your life?

4. Read Numbers 11.

   a. What did the Israelites grumble about? (Numbers 11:1–6)

   b. Do you find their complaints surprising? Why or why not?

   c. What were the consequences of their complaining? (Numbers 11:1–3, 18–20, 31–35)

   d. What did Moses complain about? (Numbers 11:10–15)

   e. What happened because of his complaints? (Numbers 11:16–17, 24–25)

f. Why do you think the results of Moses' complaints and the Israelites' grumbling were so different?

5. What key lesson did you learn today?

6. Write out our memory verse for this week: "Give thanks in all circumstances; for this is the will of God in Christ Jesus for you" (1 Thessalonians 5:18). To help you memorize this passage, write it in the space below.

Meaningful Makeover

Try a No-Complaining Challenge today. Determine not to let any grumbling or whining words escape your mouth. Were you able to meet the challenge? If not, why did you complain? Here or in your journal, write about why you sometimes grumble.

Complain to the Manufacturer

I pour out my complaint before Him; I tell my trouble before Him. Psalm 142:2

It all started with a box of dishwasher detergent. We bought a new box of the stuff and soon began noticing a change in our dishes. I grumbled to my husband that our brightly colored plastic tumblers were no longer brightly colored. Instead, they looked like the surface had been etched or sanded. I thought perhaps the formula of the offending detergent was too high in abrasives.

I called the company to complain, hoping that I would not only get my money back for the offending detergent, but also for my ruined glasses. (Never mind that these plastic tumblers were almost twenty years old. It was the principle of the thing.)

✞ *If I were to say "God, why me?" about the bad things, then I should have said "God, why me?" about the good things that happened in my life.*
Arthur Ashe[22]

The pleasant customer service representative asked that I send a sample of the detergent to the manufacturer along with some of the tumblers. I was certain that the company would acknowledge the problem and send us money to buy new glasses. However, what we received back in the mail was our own cardboard box with the old tumblers in them. Only now they were as bright and vivid as before the problem detergent. Inside the box was an explanation that the company had not found the tumblers to be scratched, merely coated with a soap scum. They had soaked the dishes in a mildly acidic solution and the gray film was now removed. I felt a little silly for complaining about soap scum, but I was glad to have the problem solved even if I didn't get my twenty-year-old tumblers replaced for free.

Simply griping about the lousy new dish detergent to my husband did nothing to fix the problem. But complaining to the manufacturer did. I needed to take my complaints to the right person.

King David knew this as well. He wrote in Psalm 142:

> With my voice I cry out to the LORD; with my voice I plead
> for mercy to the LORD. I pour out my complaint before Him; I
> tell my trouble before Him. (vv. 1–2)

"Now wait a minute!" I can hear you say. "King David, a man after God's own heart, was complaining? Isn't that what got the Israelites into so much trouble?"

Yes, but there's a difference. Let's compare what the Book of Numbers says about the Israelites' grumbling to David's words. Numbers 11:1 says, "The people complained in the hearing of the LORD." That little phrase, "in the hearing of the LORD" implies that they were kvetching among themselves, completely forgetting that God heard everything they said. They were like me complaining about the faded tumblers to my husband. He is very handy around the house, but has not been known to whip up a batch of dishwasher detergent.

King David, however, went straight to God. He poured out his complaint to the One who cares. When David approached God with his problems, he went directly to the Manufacturer to get things straightened out.

Instead of Complaining

When you feel like complaining, whining, griping, or grumbling, here are some alternatives:

• Discuss a situation with which you are dissatisfied. Complaining only expresses your frustration. Discussing tries to find a cause and solution.

• Ask for help. Sometimes I complain that no one is helping me. But did I ask anyone for assistance? Politely request help when you need it.

• Distance yourself from chronic complainers. Spending time with these people usually gets our inner griper going.

• Voice positive comments. Don't just speak up when things go wrong, talk about the things that go right!

• Determine if what you are complaining about is something you can change. Focus on the things that you can alter. Let go of things beyond your control.

God is definitely displeased when we complain about our lives "behind His back," effectively displaying displeasure with His provision and grace. But if we come to Him directly and pour out our concerns honestly, He can reassure us of His love and goodness.

Like David, I have had times when I wanted to "pour out my complaint before the LORD." Last summer, I ended up having a gripe session with God while I was driving across the state of Illinois on my way to a speaking engagement in Iowa. For months, my heart had been aching for my daughter and her family who are living in China. I was missing them terribly and took the opportunity of being alone in a car for three hours to let God know what I thought about the situation. "God, why would You give me a daughter to raise without so much as a warning that You would someday call her to a mission on the other side of the world?" I complained that it wasn't fair; "Other grandmothers have their grandchildren in the same city. Is it too much to ask to have mine in the same *country?*"

A Word of Thanksgiving for Today

Thank You, Father, for being the God who cares. I am grateful that You hear my cries.

That probably doesn't sound like a very spiritual thing for a speaker to do on her way to telling others about Jesus' love. But in pouring out my complaints, an amazing thing happened. I made room for God. Caryn Dahlstrand Rivadeneira writes in her book *Grumble Hallelujah*, "Grieving, shedding tears, emptying ourselves of hurt seems to clear up room for God to work."[23] And that's exactly what happened. By grieving for my idea of how my life should go, I allowed God to change me. By pouring out my complaints during that journey, I not only reached my destination in Iowa, but I also arrived at a place where I could see God's goodness again. Perhaps I still can't rejoice that four people I love dearly are living way out of arm's reach, but I can praise God that He will always be with us.

Look at the end of Psalm 142:

> Bring me out of prison, that I may give thanks to Your name!
> The righteous will surround me, for You will deal bountifully
> with me. (v. 7)

Being a chronic complainer can put you in a prison of discontent. But pouring out your complaints before God with the expectation that He is going to do something wonderful frees your spirit. When you believe in a God who is able to change your situation or lead you through it, you begin to live gratefully. So take your complaints straight to the Manufacturer and watch Him work!

> *Precious Lord, sometimes my life is a mess. In fact, right now there are some problems that I wish would just go away. I thank You that I can pour out my heart to You and dump all these troubles at Your feet. I can trust You with my difficulties because You are loving, You are good, and You are strong. I'm going to sit back and watch You work! Amen.*

DAY 2

Lipstick Lesson

1. When have you complained about a product or a service? What was the result?

2. In Psalm 142, David poured out his complaint to the Lord, then ended with words of praise. Check out these psalms and summarize David's words to the Lord at the beginning and the end.

Beginning	End
Psalm 6:1–3	Psalm 6:9–10
Psalm 22:1–2	Psalm 22:26–31
Psalm 64:1	Psalm 64:7–10
Psalm 69:1–3	Psalm 69:30–36

How can David's words help you when you feel like complaining?

3. What key lesson did you learn today?

4. Write out our memory verse for this week: "Give thanks in all circumstances; for this is the will of God in Christ Jesus for you" (1 Thessalonians 5:18). Read a phrase, then cover it and write it. Recite as much of the verse as you can without looking.

Meaningful Makeover

Using the psalms you read today as a model, write a psalm of complaint. Pour out your heart to Him; don't be afraid to honestly express your feelings. But remember to end with a confession of your trust that God will work everything out for your good. Praise Him for His goodness, love, and strength.

DAY 3

Toilet-Seat Gifts

Give thanks in all circumstances; for this is the will of God in Christ Jesus for you. 1 Thessalonians 5:18

An intriguing package under the Christmas tree teased me. Red and green wrapping paper. Obvious oval shape. My name on the gift tag. What was my creative husband up to now?

It was the year we were building a new house, so I suspected that the curiously wrapped package was an oval picture frame. I imagined opening the present and finding an oak frame encircling a photo of our family. I envisioned it hanging in the living room of our new home. I knew it would be beautiful.

As our family sat around the twinkling tree taking turns opening presents, I grabbed the oval package, flashed a knowing smile at my husband, ripped off the Christmas paper and discovered . . . a toilet seat!

My silence told my disappointment. Certainly, a toilet seat was a necessary item for the new house, but I couldn't hang it in my living room, could I? It was made of oak, but wasn't designed to hold a family photo. Although it was a "deluxe model," a toilet seat was not my idea of a deluxe Christmas present.

My husband broke the silence with laughter and said, "It's a joke."

I responded with an anemic "Ha-ha." Then I mumbled "Thanks," and we moved on to the next present.

Just as I didn't know how to react when I received that Christmas joke present, I often don't know how to respond when life sends me toilet-seat gifts. When I receive something totally unexpected, something definitely not on my wish list, I want to ask God, "Are you kidding? Is this some kind of joke? Do you expect me to be thankful for this?"[24]

✟ *In normal life one is often not at all aware that we always receive infinitely more than we give and that gratitude is what enriches life.*
Dietrich Bonhoeffer[25]

Like everyone else, I've had experiences I wish God had edited out of my life: deaths of loved ones, challenging relationships, children with serious illnesses. One day when one of these toilet-seat gifts dropped in my lap, I was reading 1 Thessalonians 5. The words there made me cringe, "Give thanks in all circumstances; for this is the will of God in Christ Jesus for you" (v. 18).

I wanted to yell, "God, how can you expect me to thank you for this!" But then I noticed that Paul didn't instruct me to give thanks *for* all circumstances, he said, "Be thankful in all circumstances." Even when I couldn't bring myself to thank God for the hard times, I could be grateful for His love, His comfort, and His peace in those painful situations.

I'm sure you've had toilet-seat gifts in your life too. Pesky little problems that made you want to grumble. Serious situations that made you want to scream out at God. Dreadful circumstances that inspired anything but a thankful heart.

Cultivate a Gratitude Attitude

The best way to develop complaint restraint is to cultivate a gratitude attitude. But just like any skill, learning a thankful mind-set does take some practice. Here are some ways to develop a habit of gratefulness:

• Use visual reminders. Put up sticky notes with gratitude Scriptures or quotes.

• Think of the mundane. My mood will instantly lift when I remember to express thankfulness for the little things that make my life better: my microwave, my soft, fluffy robe, and dark chocolate!

• Avoid comparisons. When I compare my life to someone else's, I can easily find something to complain about. But if I focus on my blessings, gratitude flows instead.

• Keep a list of your most precious blessings. Put the list in your purse or post it on your refrigerator. When you feel like complaining, look at your inventory of blessings.

• Make dinner time a gratitude session. Have everyone at the table tell about one thing they are grateful for that day.

The gift of pain and heartache doesn't look very attractive. The wrapping is dark, the packaging is repulsive. But look inside unwanted gifts and thank God that He is able to craft treasure out of misery. Learn to thank Him in advance for the unseen riches, the invaluable instruction or the indispensable mind-set that will come from your current circumstances.

A Word of Thanksgiving for Today

Thank You, Lord, that You are able to fashion purpose from pain and treasure from trouble.

Sometimes, the blessing will be a physical benefit. When my friend Chris needed an emergency appendectomy, she didn't think she was fortunate. But Chris ended up thanking God for the surgery because it saved her life. During the appendectomy, the early stages of colon cancer were discovered. She was treated and is now cancer free.

Other times the benefit will be a spiritual one. While Barb's children were still small, she was hospitalized for heart problems. She was distraught about her health and the care of her children. In the middle of her anxious feelings, she finally came to the point where she decided to thank God for her heart problems and the hospitalization. She knew God was in control and could bring good out of even this serious situation. Because of her thankful attitude, she experienced peace and her health improved. She credits that incident with a lifelong attitude of trust in God's care.

✞ *We should call upon His name in every trouble, pray, praise, and give thanks. (Luther's Small Catechism)*

When I received that original toilet-seat gift, I didn't like it—not even as a joke. But that gift started a yearly tradition of Christmas gag gifts and an annual source of laughter. My sarcastic "thanks" to my husband that Christmas eventually became a sincere expression of gratitude for adding so much hilarity to our lives.

And now when life presents me with a toilet-seat gift and I want to yell, "Are you kidding? Be grateful for *this?*" I try to remember to give thanks in all circumstances. This gratitude changes my perspective. Thanksgiving nourishes my trust in my heavenly Father's goodness and providence. When toilet-seat gifts appear in my life, heartfelt thankfulness changes me.

> *Gracious Father, when life gives gifts of pain and heartache, I don't feel like saying "thank You." When these tough times come, give me eyes to see the blessings beneath the dark wrapping. Give me a heart of gratitude. In Jesus' name. Amen.*

DAY 3

1. Have you received any "toilet-seat gifts" from friends or family? Describe the gift and your reaction.

2. Psalm 107 is a history of the people of Israel. Read the psalm, noting the refrain in verses 8, 15, 21, and 31. Try your hand at writing a psalm, recording how God has worked in your life. Include Psalm 107's refrain after every "chapter" of your life.

3. What key lesson did you learn today?

4. Write out this week's memory verse. Try not to peek!

Meaningful Makeover

Viewing life through the rearview mirror often allows us to see the good that resulted from a tough time. Think back to a difficult period in your life and write down any benefits that came about because of it. Write a prayer praising His ability to bring about good from even the worst of circumstances.

DAY 4

The Choice of Gratitude

Oh give thanks to the LORD, for He is good; for His steadfast love endures forever! Psalm 118:1

Barb was doubtful. Could a gratitude journal actually help? Would writing out thankful prayers make any difference in her life?

Barb and I were both members of a Bible study group named Sisters in Christ. One month, a leader of the group challenged us to keep gratitude journals. She asked us to record three things we were grateful for each day. A couple of weeks into the assignment, Barb shared the dramatic difference this simple exercise had accomplished. She admitted that she had been skeptical that a gratitude journal would change anything in her stressful life. But she discovered that thanking God for the good things even in the midst of difficult times had definitely increased her joy.

This kind of gratitude is a choice. It is not the thankful feeling that spontaneously bubbles out of the heart when everything is going right. It is purposefully looking for the good in life, acknowledging it, and then expressing thankfulness. And admittedly, this is easier some days than others.

Did You Know?

Lip gloss was invented by Max Factor in 1930. He created the product to make actresses' lips appear shiny in black and white films. But soon other women were clamoring for the product. Max Factor satisfied the public with a commercially available lip gloss in 1932.[26]

I dug out my own gratitude journal from that Bible study group. Some days, my thank-you prayers were for pretty obvious things: my terrific husband, my fantastic daughter, and my wonderful son. Other days, I recorded grateful prayers for beautiful, yet fleeting things: the pale shade of green on the trees in spring, the magnolia tree in full bloom down the street, the good laugh shared at Bible study.

But one day, I couldn't even come up with three things. I wrote:

Thank You, Lord, that You love me even when I'm in a bad mood.

I don't remember what was going on that day, but I guess the gratitude journal helped because the next day I did find three things to be thankful for, one of which was the way the air smells after it rains.

Barb and I are not the only ones to discover that gratitude journals can improve your attitude. In fact, academic studies have shown how gratitude can enhance your life. Dr. Robert Emmons, professor at University of California, Davis, has done extensive research in this area. He writes in his book *Thanks: How the New Science of Gratitude Can Make You Happier*:

> Gratitude elevates, it energizes, it inspires, it transforms.
> People are moved, opened, and humbled through experiences
> and expressions of gratitude. Gratitude provides life with
> meaning by encapsulating life itself as a gift. Without
> gratitude, life can be lonely, depressing, impoverished.[27]

Benefits of Gratitude

According to Dr. Robert Emmons, people who regularly practice gratitude:

- Exercise more regularly
- Are more optimistic about the future
- Feel more loving and forgiving
- Cope with stress more effectively
- Report greater work productivity
- Feel closer to God[28]

Through his research, Emmons found that people who regularly practice thankful thinking reap both emotional and physical benefits. His studies concluded that grateful people suffer fewer illnesses and are able to recover more quickly from any sicknesses they do have. People who keep gratitude journals experience greater joy and enthusiasm for life. They have close relationships and feel connected to other people.

The results of Emmons's studies are amazing. And yet he does not include a benefit of thanksgiving that I have discovered in my own life: Gratitude opens my heart. When I am complaining, I am clenching tightly to my idea of how life should be. I'm miffed that things are not going according to Sharla's Plan. Complaining keeps me stuck in my funk because I am unwilling to open my mind to something better. I'm a little like a contestant on *Let's Make a Deal*, holding onto my original idea of happiness, unwilling to trade for what is behind Door Number 3.

A Word of Thanksgiving for Today

Thank You, Father, that Your plan for my life is more wonderful than anything I could ever envision.

But when I begin to thank God for the good in my life, even if circumstances are not perfect, I begin to loosen my grip on Sharla's Plan. In my gratitude, I recognize that everything good in my life is a gift from God, and therefore, what God has in mind for my future is infinitely better than anything I could design. Thankfulness for God's current blessings helps me to see that exchanging my original idea of happiness for what God has for me behind Door Number 3 carries no risk for disappointment.

Psalm 118:1 explains why giving thanks should be easy, why trusting God should be effortless:

> Oh give thanks to the LORD, for He is good; for His steadfast love endures forever!

God is good. Life may be mean and rotten, but God is not. He is pure, blameless, and generous. He wants to give us His very best.

God is loving. He is tender, kind, and generous. Our heavenly Father genuinely cares about each of us. He is devoted to our eternal welfare.

✝ *Gratitude opens my heart to see that exchanging my original idea of happiness for God's plan carries no risk for disappointment.*

When I stop complaining long enough to remember these things, I begin to perceive previously unnoticed blessings. I am able to move beyond my disappointment and start to see new opportunities for joy. I find it easier to trust that whatever God has hidden behind the curtain of my future will be amazing.

When we make the choice to abandon words in the shade of Whining Wine and wear the gloss of thanksgiving, we will gain many benefits. Research shows gratefulness achieves both physical and emotional advantages. But the greatest gain is that gratitude opens our hearts to God's plan for our lives.

Loving Father, forgive me when my complaining closes my eyes to Your goodness. Give me vision to see the blessings You have already given me and joyful expectation to anticipate what You have planned for my future. Today I choose gratitude. In Jesus' name. Amen.

STEP 6

DAY 4

Lipstick Lesson

1. Are you surprised by the benefits of gratitude? Which benefit do you find most remarkable?

2. Read Psalm 50.

   a. In verses 7–15, God is speaking to His people. What does God say about sacrifices in this passage?

   b. Verses 16–21 address "the wicked." How do these people demonstrate their need for a Mouth Makeover?

   c. According to verse 22, why did the wicked do these things? How does our view of God affect our behavior?

   d. Reread verse 23. In your opinion, how do thank offerings honor God?

4. What key lesson did you learn today?

5. Write out this week's memory verse. No peeking!

Meaningful Makeover

Write down three things you are thankful for today. Consider beginning a gratitude journal. You might discover it radically transforms your life.

Thank You, Father

And Jesus lifted up His eyes and said, "Father, I thank You that You have heard Me." John 11:41

What a day! It began in sorrow and disappointment. Lazarus, my brother was gone and Jesus, our friend, had not arrived in time to help. My sister Mary and I did not understand what could have kept Him away.

When Jesus finally did arrive today, I wanted to demand an answer. I wanted to march up to Him, pound my fists on His chest, and ask, "Why didn't You come sooner?"

But when I saw His face, I knew He felt the death of Lazarus too, and I couldn't confront Him. His own eyes filled with tears when Mary crumpled at His feet in grief. As He held His tear-stained face in His hands, I knew that at least we had a Friend who understood our sorrow.

But Jesus did more than comfort. At first, I didn't understand what He was doing when He asked to go to the tomb. I thought: He also needs to grieve.

He instructed some of the men to remove the stone from the cave opening. My mind questioned His logic: Lazarus had been dead for days. It would not smell like sweet jasmine if we opened the tomb. I tried to remind Him of this fact, but He insisted.

Jesus lifted His gaze to heaven to pray. Yes, I thought, a prayer. We all need to pray.

"Thank You, Father." Jesus began. *Thank You, Father?* What could Jesus possibly thank God for at this time?

"Thank You, Father, that You have heard Me." Of course, the Father heard Jesus. But how was that helpful right now?

I was still puzzled, but my bewilderment turned to astonished joy, because Jesus soon shouted into the tomb, "Lazarus, come out!"

I couldn't imagine a happier ending to the day. Lazarus came out! My brother is alive! Jesus answered our pleas with a miracle.

When I read the story of the death of Lazarus, I wonder if Martha or Mary wanted to complain. Did the sisters want to criticize Jesus' timing or protest His delay? Were they even tempted to question His love for them? After all, He had spent time with them. They had enjoyed meals and conversations together, and yet He had not come when they needed Him most.

And Jesus, did He also feel like complaining? We know that He always did the will of the Father (John 4:34). Did His human side want to protest the Father's plan for Lazarus? A plan that would mean sickness for a friend and four days of intense grief for the sisters?

Jesus could have complained—about many things. He gave up a place without pain to live in a world full of the stuff. He left a home where He was worshiped to live where He was ridiculed. He abandoned glory for agonizing death on a cross.

✝ *I would maintain that thanks are the highest form of thought, and that gratitude is happiness doubled by wonder. G.K. Chesterton[29]*

But in the Gospels, we never read that Jesus complained about hunger or lack of sleep or sore feet. He didn't gripe about the hot sun or the pressing crowds. Perhaps the closest Jesus came to complaining was criticizing the disciples' wimpy faith (Matthew 16:8) or cursing a fig tree with no figs (Matthew 21:19).

Even in Bethany, at a time of great sorrow, we do not see Jesus complaining. What we do see is that He gave thanks.

We know that Jesus felt deep grief. The verse known by every Sunday School student and famous for its brevity is in the middle of this story: "Jesus wept" (John 11:35). Perhaps Jesus cried because He knew the pain that His friend Lazarus had endured before he died. Maybe Jesus' grief was a sympathetic sorrow as He felt the hurt in Mary and Martha's hearts. Possibly His tears resulted from the knowledge of His own imminent death.

Whatever the reason for Jesus' grief, He did something a little surprising in the midst of it. He gave thanks. Offering a prayer of gratitude in a time of loss is not an easy thing to do. But Jesus modeled this behavior for us.

And I love Jesus' prayer: "Father, I thank You that You have heard Me" (John 11:41). Jesus prayed that prayer so the people around Him would understand exactly who He was, but it happens to be an excellent prayer of gratitude when thanksgiving is difficult.

✝ *When we don't feel like thanking God for the events in our lives, we can still thank Him that our prayers never go to voice mail.*

It's a prayer we all can pray. God is waiting to hear our cries too. He is leaning forward to listen to our petitions. And when we don't feel like we can thank God for anything else, we can thank Him for that. When it is difficult to be grateful for the events in our lives, we can still thank God that He never puts us on hold. Even if we feel like complaining about God's timing, we can still appreciate the fact that our prayers never go to voice mail.

In our humanness, we often feel like complaining. We want to whine when the weather is lousy and gripe when the server at Denny's is slow. We want to grumble when life hands us toilet-seat gifts. But when those complaints begin to form in our mouths, let's try applying the gloss of thanksgiving. Let's thank the Father that He offers to be the sounding board for our complaints if we will come to Him in trust. Live a life of gratitude and open your hearts to God's plan.

A Word of Thankfulness for Today

Thank You, Father, that You are leaning close to hear me. Thank You that You not only hear every cry of joy and shout of praise, but also every whisper of despair and sob of grief.

Thank You, Father, that You hear me. Thank You, Father, that Your ears are always tipped toward earth, ready to listen to me. Thank You that I never have to wait in line to talk to You, never have to wonder if You received my call. When I feel like complaining, help me remember this: You are here. You are listening. In Jesus' name. Amen.

DAY 5

Lipstick Lesson

1. We've been talking about wearing the gloss of thankfulness on our lips this week. How could wearing this "lip product" affect your appearance? your witness to nonbelievers? your outlook on life?

STEP 6

2. Read the story of Lazarus's death in John 11:1–44. Imagine yourself as Mary or Martha. Describe your emotions as you watch Jesus in front of the tomb.

3. LIP Study

To learn more about thankful speech, let's apply the three-step LIP process to Isaiah 12. Read through the passage three times and follow these steps (I have done a few for you as examples):

Look for the Facts

Interpret the Meaning

Pursue the Application

Look for the facts. Don't make any interpretations here. Simply write what is happening in each verse.

Verse 1 I will praise You, Lord. You were angry with me, but now You have comforted me.

Verse 2 I will trust and not be afraid because God is my salvation, strength, and song.

Verse 3

Verse 4

Verse 5

Verse 6

Interpret the meaning. Turn the lesson in the passage into a scriptural principle.

Verse 1 Praising God is a choice. (I will praise You, Lord.)

Verse 2 Because God is strong and mighty, I have no reason to be afraid.

Verse 3

Verse 4

Verse 5

Verse 6

Pursue the application. Turn the principle you discovered into a personal question that applies the truth to your life.

Verse 1 Do I make a conscious choice to praise God even when I don't feel like it?

Verse 2 Do I feel fear or anxiety today? How can I remind myself of God's saving strength?

Verse 3

Verse 4

Verse 5

Verse 6

4. What key lesson did you learn today?

5. Write 1 Thessalonians 5:18 from memory.

Meaningful Makeover

Choose one question from those you posed in "Pursue the Application." In the space here or in your journal, write your honest answer and come up with an action you can do to grow in that area.

STEP 7

Seal: Protect with Discretion

Memory Verse

For everything there is a season, and a time for every matter under heaven: . . . a time to keep silence, and a time to speak. Ecclesiastes 3:1, 7b

Quiet?

Whoever restrains his words has knowledge, and he who has a cool spirit is a man of understanding. Even a fool who keeps silent is considered wise; when he closes his lips, he is deemed intelligent. Proverbs 17:27–28

When my nephew was three, he didn't understand what the word *quiet* meant. This became very evident when he spent a week at our house. My sister Shelly called to ask if we could watch Seth while they drove to West Virginia for a funeral. I quickly agreed. I knew that playing with his cousins would be a lot more fun for Seth than going to the funeral of an uncle he had never met.

My own kids were eleven and eight at the time and were able to entertain him quite a bit, even when I was occupied with teaching piano lessons. The only trouble was that Seth had not yet learned how to use his "inside" voice. Although I taught piano lessons in the living room—which was on the opposite end of the house from the family room where he was playing—I could hear his voice. My children would try to softly tell Seth, "Quiet." And Seth would shout, "QUIET?" Apparently, it was a foreign concept to him.

We finally gave up, and I would just greet my piano students with an explanation of the situation and ask them to excuse my houseguest who seemed to have no understanding of quiet.

A Quiet Word for Today
The Holy Spirit whispers God's truth into our hearts.

Sometimes I'm like that too. I think of something to say. The Holy Spirit whispers, "Quiet." But I ignore Him and blurt it out anyway. I'm reckless with my speech, thoughtless with my words.

A lip sealer is an invisible coating you apply over your lipstick to prevent it from smudging. Often, my mouth could use protection like this to stop hasty words. Progress in my Mouth Makeover means I will learn discretion. Wearing a spiritual lip sealer means knowing when to speak and when to keep quiet.

✞ *I seldom feel sorry for the things I did not say. Author unknown*[30]

God's Word talks about knowing when to be silent. Proverbs 17:27 tells us, "Whoever restrains his words has knowledge, and he who has a cool spirit is a man of understanding." The Hebrew word for restrain is *chasak*, which can be translated as: "to hold back or to keep in check." Not every word that enters our minds needs to come out of our mouths. Some need to be restrained.

According to Proverbs, the key to restraint is knowledge. In the Hebrew, the word for knowledge is *da`ath*, which means not only knowledge, but discernment. To discern is to "see or understand the difference; to make distinction; as to discern between good and evil, truth and falsehood."[31] To be discerning in our speech is to make a distinction between what words should be expressed and which should be left unsaid.

Think of discernment like a coffee filter. The filter holds back the grounds and lets the coffee through. Without the filter, you end up with a gritty, bitter cup of java.

When we use the filter of discernment, we strain out the hurtful, angry, and gossipy words. But we allow the encouraging words, praising words, and thankful words to flow. Without discernment, we may end up with rough times in our relationships and bitter people in our lives.

At this point in our study, we know what should be strained out of our conversations. Words of slander or gossip should be held back. Boasting is banned. Lies and untruths are to be avoided. Nagging is prohibited. Complaining and whining words need to be filtered from our vocabularies.

We want to do this. If you are reading this book, you have a desire to please God with your speech. You want your words to positively influence your world.

Yet we are frustrated when our word filter leaks. We are discouraged when once again we have let negative words slip out of our mouths. How can we practice discernment in our speech?

The first step is to perceive. Gather more information about the person you are speaking to before you say something you will regret. Before you make a statement, find out more about the situation. Ask yourself, "What don't I know?" That way you won't tell a fellow party attendee that you think the food is awful only to find out you are speaking to the husband of the caterer.

Lip Sealer of Discretion

Use these three questions daily to develop discretion:

- Is what I'm about to say necessary?

- Is it kind?

- Is it something I would say if Jesus were sitting next to me?

The second step in filtering our speech is to pause. Proverbs 29:20 says: "Do you see a man who is hasty in his words? There is more hope for a fool than for him." Before you speak, wait a moment. Weigh your words. Think about the effect they will have. Will they bring joy or pain?

The third step in learning discernment is to pray. In that pause before you speak, offer up a quick prayer. Pray for sensitivity to the situation. Ask God, "Does this need to be said?" Listen for His answer.

Begin each day asking God for His lip sealer to prevent hasty words. Pray for discretion in your speech and wisdom in knowing when to speak and when to keep quiet. As you go through your day, pay attention to God's voice. Before you spout an opinion, tell a joke, or spew out a complaint, listen. Is God whispering, "Quiet"?

DAY 1

Lipstick Lesson

1. Lip sealers prevent lipstick from smudging. Don't you hate it when your lipstick comes off on your coffee cup? What do you do to keep your lipstick on your lips?

2. Review the three questions for developing discretion in our speech (pp. 169–170). Which one will be most helpful to you this week? Why?

3. According to the following verses, what kind of words should we hold back?
   a. Exodus 20:7
   b. Proverbs 11:12
   c. Proverbs 11:13
   d. 2 Timothy 2:16

4. What key lesson did you learn today?

5. Write out our memory verse for this week: "For everything there is a season, and a time for every matter under heaven: . . . a time to keep silence, and a time to speak" (Ecclesiastes 3:1, 7b). To help you memorize this passage, write it out in the space below.

Meaningful Makeover

On an index card, write out the three questions on page 168 under "Lip Sealer of Discretion." Post the card in a prominent place in your home or office to remind you to use discretion in your speech today. Journal about your words.

Slow to Speak, Slow to Anger

Know this, my beloved brothers: let every person be quick to hear,
slow to speak, slow to anger. James 1:19

Slow to anger. Happily, this expression fits my pastor husband like a well-tailored clerical shirt. I've never seen him lose his temper. John is rarely annoyed and seldom cross. However, when we were first married, I discovered that on the few occasions when he was angry, he was also slow to speak. Whenever John was upset about something, he would become very quiet.

This was terribly frustrating to me. I like to talk about my feelings and bare my soul. I couldn't understand his silence. How could we change the situation if we didn't discuss it?

What I didn't realize then was that John had grown up with a father who gave full vent to his anger—loudly and often. John was striving to avoid his father's mistakes. Sometimes that meant he had to be slow to speak in order to not express his anger in a harmful way.

I thank John for his silence. Although those quiet times were uncomfortable, I realize now that angry words would have been much more painful. Hurtful words could have left lasting bruises. My wise husband realized we can never erase the words we have spoken, so he was careful with his speech.

> ✝ *Speak when you are angry and you'll make the best speech*
> *you'll ever regret. Ambrose Bierce*[32]

James wrote in his epistle, "Let every person be quick to hear, slow to speak, slow to anger" (James 1:19). Perhaps the most important time to apply lip sealer to our mouths is when we are infuriated. Somehow the strong emotions of anger breed the most wounding words. Rage can uncork words that later we wish we had left unsaid.

A Quiet Word for Today

The Lord is never quick to release His anger. He is patient and compassionate.

But eventually we must talk. Sooner or later, the issue must be discussed. So how can we discover the right words to use when there is disagreement? How can discretion help us to choose the best words for the situation?

Here are some guidelines I found from the Book of Proverbs:

Ask yourself, "Why am I so angry?" When I read Proverbs 13:10, "Pride only breeds quarrels" (NIV), I realized that many times my anger is rooted in pride. I am convinced my plan is best. I want things done my way. I'm not even trying to see the other person's point of view. Examining the source of my anger may reveal that I really don't have a good reason to be angry. Or it may lead to an honest discussion of each person's perspective of the situation.

Anger is also often rooted in fear or hurt. Is your rage due to financial fear or anxiety about the relationship? Are you furious because of someone else's wounding words? Try to pinpoint exactly what is upsetting you.

Calm Communication Course

Instead of angry words, try these communication techniques:

- Begin with prayer. Ask God to help you work things out.

- Before giving criticism, offer affirmation. Tell the other person something you appreciate about them.

- Use "I" statements. "I feel hurt when you . . ." "I get angry when you . . ."

- Concentrate on the issue. Discuss one problem at a time. Don't bring up every past conflict.

- Try to see the other person's perspective. Look for points you can agree on.

Ask yourself, "What is the best way to talk about this problem?" Proverbs 15:1 says, "A soft answer turns away wrath, but a harsh word stirs up anger." I need to think through my words before I speak. Gentle speech will be more effective. Yelling and shouting only exacerbate the problem.

Sometimes journaling is a helpful tool to use when angry. Writing your thoughts about the situation can cool your emotions. It might even help in discovering the real source of your anger. Journaling may help you clarify your thoughts and give you the ability to discuss the issue more calmly.

However, it is usually not best to use the written word to tell the other person about your anger. A letter can seem cold and callous. Discuss the problem in person whenever possible. Establish eye contact and use a calm tone of voice.

✝ *God forbids us to keep anger and hatred in our hearts against our neighbor.*
(Luther's Small Catechism)

Ask God for a pressure valve. Proverbs 29:11 says, "A fool gives full vent to his spirit, but a wise man quietly holds it back." One day when I was a newly-wed, I decided to cook dinner using one of our wedding gifts—a pressure cooker. I had been learning about the benefits of a vegetarian diet in my nutrition class, and I determined that we were going to try soybeans. My vegetarian cookbook said that a pressure cooker was the fastest way to cook them. I followed the directions for the correct amounts of water and soybeans, put on the lid, and popped the pressure valve on top. I turned on the burner and waited for the beans to cook. It wasn't long before the pressure cooker began to make alarming noises—noises I had never heard before. I ran to turn off the heat, but I was too late. The pressure valve flew off the kettle and the soybeans sprayed all over the ceiling. I was terribly upset about the mess, but I think John was secretly happy he didn't have to eat the soybeans.

When we are angry, our own pressure valves may also be faulty. Sometimes it's difficult not to spew all of our messy words into the room. But God can re-place the valve and prevent an eruption of rage. Let's ask God to help us not give full vent to our anger. Pray for the wisdom to know what should be expressed and what should be held back.

Although those soybeans were eventually removed from the ceiling, the words that escape our lips can never be taken back. Remember the lip sealer of discretion whenever angry words threaten to burst from your lips. Avoid harm-ing others with your mouth. Be slow to speak and slow to anger.

> *God of peace, forgive me when my angry words hurt Your children. Help me to learn to be slow to speak and slow to anger. Give me wisdom to choose words that can resolve conflict without bruising others. In Jesus' name. Amen.*

DAY 2

Lipstick Lesson

1. When you are angry, are you more likely to speak your mind or hold it in? What are the results?

2. Read Ephesians 4:26–27.

   a. It is interesting to note that anger is an emotion and not necessarily sinful in and of itself. How can we express anger and not sin?

   b. What is the principle behind the phrase "Do not let the sun go down on your anger"?

   c. Do you always follow Paul's advice to not let the sun go down on your anger? Why or why not?

   d. The NIV translates verse 27 as "do not give the devil a foothold." The ESV says "Give no opportunity to the devil." How can persistent anger give Satan an advantage over you?

3. What key lesson did you learn today?

4. Write out this week's memory verse: "For everything there is a season, and a time for every matter under heaven: . . . a time to keep silence, and a time to speak" (Ecclesiastes 3:1, 7b). Read a phrase, then cover it and write it. Recite as much of it as you can without looking.

Meaningful Makeover

Are you struggling with anger right now? Take some time to journal your feelings. Ask God to pinpoint what you are actually angry about. Pray for the right words to talk about the problem.

If anger is not currently a problem, ask yourself, "What did I learn today that can help me when I am experiencing conflict?" Write down two or three things that you want to remember for the future.

The Art of Listening

He who answers before listening—that is his folly and his shame. Proverbs 18:13 NIV

Every Sunday, my twenty-three-year-old son picks up his grandmother, Shirley, from her senior apartment and brings her to church. Now, Nathaniel is one of those strong, silent types and typically not too talkative before noon. One Sunday morning, Shirley entered the church vestibule complaining that Nathaniel had not let her get a word in edgewise during her ride to church. We didn't believe her for a minute.

We all love Shirley for many reasons. I especially love her for the fact that when I'm with her I never have to think of something to say. There are never any awkward silences because my mother-in-law fills them all!

Shirley is not the only woman known for her loquacious tongue. It is estimated that women speak approximately 9,000 words per day (compared to 6,000 words per day for men).[33] Women gather in coffee shops to chat, get together in book clubs to share thoughts, and join Bible studies to speak about faith. Women love words.

The trouble with so many words is that sometimes they get in the way of real interaction and relationship. Proverbs 18:13 (NIV) tells us, "He who answers before listening—that is his folly and his shame." Genuine communication involves not only sharing my thoughts but listening to the ideas of others. One of the best ways to use our 9,000 words per day is get others talking.

My sister-in-law Kathy is especially skilled at this. She knows how to ask insightful questions that bring out the best in people. She listens attentively. She is genuinely interested in what the other person has to say.

Five Intriguing Questions to Get Others Talking

1. If you could replay any moment in your life, which one would it be?

2. What is your favorite holiday (or season)? Why?

3. What's the best surprise you've ever received?

4. What word would you say describes you best? Why?

5. If you could meet any one person, whom would you choose?

My mother is also an expert listener. My siblings and I tease her that her phone line is almost constantly busy. But when I visit her and she receives a phone call, I notice that she says very little. People call her because she listens. She gives the gift of purposeful attention.

A Quiet Word for Today

My heavenly Father is always available to listen, always ready to pay attention to my prayers.

I want to give this same gift to the people in my life, so I'm trying to learn to be a good listener as well. Experts tell us to ask an open-ended question to get people talking. Focus on the answer, and use what you have learned about the person to ask a follow-up question. Try to find a common interest between you and your conversation partner.

The more I practice the art of listening, the more enjoyable conversation becomes. When I'm intent on what the other person has to say, I don't worry about coming up with something impressive or witty to add to the dialogue. If I'm not planning my next comment while the other person is talking, I'm much more likely to learn something interesting.

One of my friends recently used the art of listening at a business function she attended with her husband. Cheryl found herself conversing with the wife of one of her husband's bosses. Since she had just met the woman, she asked questions and listened (and listened and listened). Later in the evening, the women met up with their husbands and the boss's wife told her spouse, "Cheryl is the most fascinating person I have ever met. We simply must invite her and her husband to our Italian villa!" So Cheryl, who simply sensed that this woman had deep emotional and spiritual needs, ended up with free lodgings in Italy!

Words are not our only communication tools. In a conversation I had with Loren Keller, an industrial psychologist, I learned that when we are speaking with someone, our words contribute only seven percent to what is being communicated. Ninety-three percent of our meaning comes from tone of voice and body language.

In the Book of Ecclesiastes, we read, "The *quiet* words of the wise are more to be heeded than the shouts of a ruler of fools" (Ecclesiastes 9:17 NIV, emphasis mine). What we say is important, but how we say it may determine whether people actually pay attention. When we are practicing the art of listening, can others sense genuine interest in our voices? Or does our tone betray irritation or impatience?

Have you ever had a conversation with people you were sure never heard a word you said? What gave them away? Most likely their body language betrayed them. Perhaps they kept looking toward the door or turning away. Maybe they nodded to every person that passed by. The way they used their bodies told you they simply were not interested. If we want to be caring and compassionate communicators, we will demonstrate that in our posture, eye movements, facial expressions, and gestures.

Five Positive Ways to Use Body Language

1. Maintain eye contact. Try not to glance away while the other person is talking.

2. Lean forward. This shows you are interested, not bored.

3. Open up your arms and body. Crossing your arms makes you look defensive and guarded.

4. Relax your body position. Avoid hunching your shoulders, swinging your leg, or tapping a pen.

5. Nod and smile. This gives visual clues that you are listening and the other person should continue speaking.

Sometimes a gesture is all that is needed. I love the story of the little girl who came home after visiting the neighbor who had just lost her husband. Her mother asked her, "Why did you go?"

The little girl answered, "To make her feel better."

Mom was a little curious. "How did you do that?"

The little girl said, "I crawled up on her lap and cried with her."

That wise little girl knew that words were not needed in that situation. Although what we say is important, we need to remember the message of Ecclesiastes: "There is . . . a time to keep silence, and a time to speak" (Ecclesiastes 3:1, 7b). Sometimes the best gift is a hug or a hand to hold. Henri Nouwen, a Dutch-born priest and author, wrote:

The friend who can be silent with us in a moment of despair or confusion, who can stay with us in an hour of grief and bereavement, who can tolerate not knowing . . . not healing, not curing . . . that is a friend who cares.[34]

May we have insight to know when to speak and when to be silent. May we communicate clearly not only with words but in the tone of our voices and the gestures we use. May we learn the art of listening. Let us use our daily allotment of nine thousand words wisely.

Father in heaven, You are the God who hears. Forgive me when I have spoken when I should have listened. Help me to appreciate the gift of language so I use it wisely and to Your glory. Make me sensitive to the needs of the people in my life. In Jesus' name. Amen.

DAY 3

Lipstick Lesson

1. Do you know anyone gifted in the art of listening? What makes that person a good listener?

2. The Book of Job gives a tutorial in good and bad communication techniques.

    a. Read Job 2:11–13. How do Job's friends comfort him? (If you are not familiar with what happened to Job, read Job 1.)

    b. Unfortunately, Job's friends did not stop there. Instead, their many words fill up fifteen chapters. Read Job 11:10–20 as an example of their message. What did Job's friends tell him?

    c. What is Job's response in Job 13:5?

    d. What can we learn from the example of Job's friends?

3. What key lesson did you learn today?

4. Write out this week's memory verse. Try not to peek!

Meaningful Makeover

Today, work on your listening skills. Ask purposeful questions and demonstrate interest in your nonverbal communication. Journal about your experience.

DAY 4

Be Still

"Be still, and know that I am God. I will be exalted among the nations, I will be exalted in the earth!" Psalm 46:10

Be still.

Even as you read those words, you are probably thinking, "Are you kidding? I don't have time to be still!"

I know the feeling. Here is a list of what is on my schedule this week: clean bathrooms, dust furniture, mop the hardwood floor, do laundry, teach piano lessons, attend music teachers' meeting, lead women's Bible study, practice piano for church service, rehearse with soloist, do the grocery shopping. Oh, and, of course, finish chapter seven of *Bless These Lips*.

I'm sure your schedule is just as full. If you have children at home, your to-do list is probably twice as long! Yet God tells us to be still.

Maybe you've been in motion for so long that you don't even know what it looks like to be still. You drink your morning coffee in the car, and you catch up with your mother on the phone on the way home from work. You grab something to eat between meetings, and you do your Bible study homework while waiting for your daughter's ballet class to finish. Be still? *What does that mean?*

In order to explore that concept, I am going to use a tool I learned during my college days. It is an approach to meditating Scripture that is helpful in quieting the soul and focusing your mind. Simply repeat a Bible verse emphasizing a different word each time and allow the Holy Spirit to teach you as you think about the significance of that word. As we meditate on the first phrase of Psalm 46:10, we will discover what it means to be still.

Be *still and know that I am God. Be* is a verb—an action word. Stillness will not come automatically. I need to make it happen. I once heard author Cynthia Heald speak on this verse. She explained that God's admonition to "be still" was a little like a mother telling her children to "be still" in church. She pictured a parent giving her child's shoulders a little shake to get him to settle down and pay attention. My heavenly Father commands me to be still because He knows that if I'm constantly in motion, I may never hear His voice.

Be **still** *and know that I am God.* Perhaps the first step in stillness is to take this verse literally. Sit down and tell your mind to be quiet and your body to relax. Ignore the laundry that is calling from the hamper. Don't listen to the clutter in the kitchen shouting your name. Perceive God's voice growing louder as you shut out the world's noise.

Five Ways to Agitate Your Soul

1. Schedule activities for every moment of the day.
2. Worry as much as possible.
3. Try to be in charge of your life.
4. Doubt God's goodness.
5. Refuse to accept your life as it is now.

The call to stillness is also a spiritual one. The command "be still" comes from the *Hiphil* stem of the verb *rapha*, which means "to be weak, to let go, to release." A better translation might be "to cause yourself to let go" or "let yourselves become weak." To be still is to surrender to an almighty God. To loosen our grips on our problems and let Jesus carry them. To lay down our ideas of how our lives should be arranged and trust God's plan. I know, I know—easier said than done.

Be still and **know** *that I am God.* That whole surrender thing becomes less difficult when we know to whom we are surrendering. The Hebrew word for know is *yada* which can mean "to be acquainted with or to know by experience." If God is merely an acquaintance, it may be difficult to trust Him with my heart. But the more I experience His care and concern for me, the more I am able to relax in His design for my life.

The Hebrew word *yada* can also mean "to recognize or admit."[35] God is God whether I recognize that fact or not. But my peace dwindles when I refuse to admit God's sovereignty. My heart is anything but quiet when I deny Jesus is Lord.

Be still and know that **I** *am God.* God is God and I am not. Intellectually I know this, but too often I act like I am God and He is not. I become intent on my plan for my life. It's when I fight against God's will that I lose the quiet in my heart. It's when I wish for some other pattern to my life than the one that is given that I relinquish stillness. Peace returns when I remember I am not God.

A Quiet Word for Today

Stillness comes when I rest in God's trustworthiness, lean on His faithfulness, and relax in His goodness.

Be still and know that I **am** *God. Am* is the present tense of the verb *to be.* Our heavenly Father does not say "I was God" or "I will be God." God is not only a God of the past who performed miracles in Bible times. Nor is He only a God of the future, waiting for the end of the world before He acts. God is God of the present. He is telling me, "I am almighty God. I am working in your life. I am calling your name."

Be still and know that I am **God.** Who is God? He is the almighty, omniscient Creator of the universe. My Father in heaven is not a wimpy god-wannabe. He is the God who loved me enough to work out a plan so I could be with Him forever. He is not a mean fairy tale ogre. God is holy, just, and good. Letting go of my heart is easier when I remember this. Quieting my soul is simpler when I contemplate God's character.

✝ *To be still is to quiet our hearts, to trust in an almighty and loving God, and to experience release as we loosen our grip on life.*

Be still and know that I am God. Be proactive in finding time to still your activity and quiet your soul. Loosen your grip on life and trust God's plan. Recognize God is in control and you only forfeit your peace when you try to deny that fact. Remember that your heavenly Father is ready to meet you right now. He is a powerful, loving, and holy God who has a magnificent design for your life.

Almighty Father, forgive me when I have been too busy to hear You call to me. Help me to still my soul in Your presence and to loosen my grip on life. Help me to live in quiet surrender to Your plan. In Jesus' name. Amen.

DAY 4

Lipstick Lesson

1. How do you quiet your soul? Talk about anything you do, from bubble baths to spiritual retreats, that brings peace to your life.

2. Try your hand at meditating on Scripture by emphasizing different words. Read Lamentations 3:19–33 (NIV) and then write your thoughts as you contemplate verse 26.

   a. It is **good** to wait quietly for the salvation of the LORD.

   b. It is good to **wait** quietly for the salvation of the LORD.

   c. It is good to wait **quietly** for the salvation of the LORD.

   d. It is good to wait quietly for the **salvation** of the LORD.

   e. It is good to wait quietly for the salvation of the **Lord.**

3. What key lesson did you learn today?

4. Write out this week's memory verse. Try not to peek!

Meaningful Makeover

Schedule time today (or this week) to still your soul in God's presence. Meditate on Scripture, tell God your concerns, listen to His voice. Journal about your experience.

DAY 5

Say Nothing

STEP 7

This they said to test Him, that they might have some charge to bring against Him. Jesus bent down and wrote with His finger on the ground. John 8:6

I strained to see the speaker. There were so many people gathered around Him that I had to stand on tiptoes just to see His face. "It's Jesus," the man in front of me whispered. Ah, Jesus. I had heard of this man. He was causing quite a stir. The synagogue officials seemed quite upset by His teaching. Perhaps this was my chance to see what all the fuss was about.

Just then, some of those synagogue officials entered the temple court and forced their way between the people to get to Jesus. They shoved a somewhat disheveled-looking woman into the center of the crowd.

"Teacher," one of the Pharisees began, "this woman has been caught in the act of adultery. Moses' Law commands us to stone such women. What do you say?"

Stone her! How could they suggest stoning? The Romans would not allow Jews to carry out an execution. Ah! I saw what these men were doing. They were trying to trap Jesus in His words. If He said they should carry out the stoning, He would be in conflict with Roman law. But if He said they shouldn't stone her, they would accuse Him of not following the Law of Moses. It was a no-win situation.

I craned my neck to see Jesus, wondering what He would say. But He said nothing. Instead, He bent over and wrote in the dirt with His finger! Perhaps the Pharisees had outfoxed Him with this question.

The Pharisees were obviously confident they had cornered Him. While Jesus continued to write in the dirt, they badgered Him, "So, which is it, Teacher?" "What do you say?" "Do we stone her or not?" Their proud talk was in stark contrast to the woman hanging her head.

Slowly, Jesus straightened up and spoke to the men, "If any one of you is without sin, let him be the first to throw a stone at her." He sat back down and drew in the dirt at His feet.

Now Jesus was not the only quiet one. The Pharisees were also silent. No more questions. No more accusations. One of the older men turned around and walked away from the crowd. Another man followed and another. Soon, only the woman was standing in the middle of the crowd.

Jesus stood up and spoke to her, "Woman, has no one stayed to condemn you?"

She said, "No one, Lord."

And Jesus told her, "Neither do I condemn you. Go and sin no more."

A Quiet Word for Today

Because I live as a baptized and forgiven daughter of the King, I daily hear Jesus' words, "Neither do I condemn you."

If you had witnessed this scene, what conclusions would you have made about Christ's silence? Would you have been perplexed when He stooped down to write in the dirt? Would you have wondered if the Pharisees had truly stumped Him?

✞ *Saying nothing . . . sometimes says the most. Emily Dickinson*[36]

Surely Jesus was not at a loss for words. He did not have to take time to think about the correct answer to the Pharisees' trick question. So why was He quiet?

Perhaps through His silence, Jesus modeled for us the need to pause before we speak. Proverbs 15:28 says, "The heart of the righteous ponders how to answer." But pondering takes time. When our mouths randomly spew out words before our brains have had time to choose the right ones, the results are often disastrous. We need to stop and think before we speak.

Can you imagine what was going through the mind of the woman as Jesus calmly drew in the dirt? The very next words He spoke could mean her death. Our words may not have life and death consequences, but they do impact the lives of others. Words can pummel hearts and batter souls. When we take the time to ponder how to answer, those words are less apt to bruise and more likely to heal.

✞ *I pray that my words will not be the product of an automatic reaction,*
but of a thoughtful response.

When Jesus did stand up and talk, He did not give a long sermon. He could have followed the Pharisees' example and pointed out all of their sins. Instead,

185

Christ gave a wise, but concise answer followed by a hush so everyone could hear their consciences speak. Sometimes, silence is the most effective communication tool.

One of the most useful tools in our spiritual makeup bag is the lip sealer of discretion. Too often I ignore this product. But I long for the quality of discrimination in my speech. Because the consequences of my words are real, it is my hope that I will learn to distinguish between which words should be expressed and which should be left unsaid. I pray that as I progress in my Mouth Makeover, I will know when it is best to say nothing.

Holy Spirit, too often my words tumble out of my mouth before my brain has thought them through. Remind me to pause and pray before I talk. Help me to speak out of understanding and wisdom of the situation. And help me to remain silent when that is the best response. In Jesus' name. Amen.

DAY 5

Lipstick Lesson

1. In the story of the adulterous woman, Jesus was silent for a while.

    a. Why do you think He was quiet?

    b. How can His example of silence help you in your conversations today?

2. LIP Study

Read the story of the adulterous woman in John 8:1–11 and use the three-step LIP process to learn more about the role of silence in our communication. Read through the passage three times and follow these steps (I have done a few for you as examples):

Look for the Facts

Interpret the Meaning

Pursue the Application

Look for the facts. Don't make any interpretations here. Simply write what is happening in each verse.

Verse 1   Jesus went to the Mount of Olives.

Verse 2   At dawn, He went to the temple courts and people gathered around to hear Him teach.

Verse 3   The scribes and Pharisees brought in a woman caught in adultery and made her stand in the middle of the group.

Verse 4

Verse 5

Verse 6

Verse 7

Verse 8

Verse 9

Verse 10

Verse 11

Interpret the meaning. Turn the lesson in the passage into a scriptural principle.

Verse 1   Even if we are busy, it is important to spend time alone with God.

Verse 2   Listen to Jesus teach in His Word and in the church.

Verse 3   Publicly accusing others of their sin is not the best first course of action.

Verse 4

Verse 5

Verse 6

Verse 7

Verse 8

Verse 9

Verse 10

Verse 11

Pursue the application. Turn the principle you discovered into a personal question that applies the truth to your life.

Verse 1   Do I yearn to spend time alone with God?

Verse 2   When I read the Bible or go to church, do I go with an attitude to learn from Jesus?

Verse 3   Do I tend to be like the judgmental Pharisees?

Verse 4

Verse 5

Verse 6

Verse 7

Verse 8

Verse 9

Verse 10

Verse 11

3. What key lesson did you learn today?

4. Write Ecclesiastes 3:1, 7b from memory.

Meaningful Makeover

Choose one question from those you posed in "Pursue the Application." In the space below or in your journal, write your honest answer and come up with an action you can do to grow in that area.

STEP 8

Smile: Share with Joy

Memory Verse

A word fitly spoken is like apples of gold in a setting of silver.
Proverbs 25:11

Spreading Sunshine, Giving Life

The mouth of the righteous is a fountain of life. Proverbs 10:11

One of my husband's responsibilities as pastor is to make monthly calls on homebound seniors. Most of the people he sees exhibit joy and faith even in their declining years. Often John comments that he is the one who leaves these visits inspired and blessed, even though it is his job to give encouragement.

However, one woman he visited often seemed to be in a foul mood. She complained that the food in the nursing home was tasteless and the nursing staff inattentive. During one of my husband's visits, this senior wondered aloud why God had left her on the earth for so long. There seemed to be no purpose for her life anymore. John tried to cheer her by saying, "God can still work through you. You can encourage the nurses, the doctors, and the aides. You could be a little ray of sunshine to everyone who comes through that door."

This senior citizen looked at him for a minute and then said, "No, pastor, that's just not me."

At least she was honest.

When the makeup expert at the cosmetics counter gave me a Mouth Makeover, she applied lip exfoliator, lip balm, lip plumper, lip liner, lip color, and lip gloss. My lips looked glamorous enough for a photo shoot. But I have to say, I do not follow that routine every day. Taking that much time with my makeup routine for something that rubs off on my coffee cup doesn't seem worth it. It just isn't me.

The Power of Lipstick

Helena Rubinstein, founder of the successful beauty company, wrote President Roosevelt asking what she could do for the war effort. The President replied with a story of a woman in London who was being carried on a stretcher during the Great Blitz. Before she allowed the medical personnel to give her a sedative, she insisted on putting on her lipstick. "It just does something for me," she explained. This story, the President explained, was proof that Helena had already done her patriotic duty.[37]

But a spiritual Mouth Makeover is another story. Although it is a lot of effort to scrub out harmful words, apply the balm of encouragement, and put on the lip plumper of praise, I take the time to do so. Although I'm still not an expert at the lip liner of truth, the gloss of thankfulness, or the lip sealer of discretion, I keep trying to get them right. Because this Mouth Makeover is worth it. We can make a difference to the people around us. We can be that ray of sunshine to the people in our lives.

A Word of Joy for Today

God's words to us are a continual source of joy. His Word in our hearts bubbles out with refreshment to others.

Proverbs 10:11 tells us, "The mouth of the righteous is a fountain of life." The Hebrew word for fountain is *maqowr*, which means "spring, fountain, and a source of life." When I was a kid, my father occasionally took my brother and me hiking up Rib Mountain, a towering peak of 1,924 feet near our home in Wausau, Wisconsin. Although it wasn't a Swiss Alp, it was a challenge for our little legs. On one of our climbs, my father stopped to point out a hole in the ground. I wasn't too impressed until my father beckoned me to come closer and I saw water was bubbling out of that hole! Dad explained that it was a spring. He dipped out some water with his hands, gulped it down, and encouraged me to do the same. The water was amazingly refreshing. The cool water on the hot day revived us, and the unexpected surprise of finding the spring gave us new energy to finish our hike up the hill.

Our words can do the same for others. An unexpected word of support can energize others on their climb through life. A clear and honest word of encouragement can refresh a soul.

When I was a preteen, I needed a word of encouragement. In sixth grade, I went through a colossal growth spurt—shooting up from 5'2" to 5'8" in just nine months. This put me in the awkward position of being taller than all of the boys in my class. I changed from a pudgy, fresh-faced kid to a gangly, pimply preteen almost overnight. I was convinced that I was certainly the ugliest girl in school.

I could have gone through the rest of my preteen years feeling self-conscious about my height if it hadn't been for one of my mother's friends. This tall and beautiful woman looked at me and understood what I was feeling. She shared that she had also hated being tall as a teenager, but in college, her height had landed her some modeling jobs. She told me not to despair—being tall could be a good thing. Those few words significantly altered my self-esteem.

> ✝ *Let encouragement bubble out of your mouth,*
> *reviving the hopeless and refreshing the disheartened.*

Sophia used her words to dramatically change her husband's life. One day, he came home with the bad news that he had lost his job. Feeling discouraged and defeated, he didn't know how Sophia would accept the situation. She surprised him with her response—"Good! Now you can write your book!"

"Yes," replied the husband, "but what will we live on?"

Sophia opened a drawer, revealing a large sum of money that she had been saving out of her housekeeping money. "You see," she explained, "I knew you were a man of genius, and that someday you would write a masterpiece. This is enough money for us to live on for a year."

That husband was Nathaniel Hawthorne and that was the year he wrote *The Scarlet Letter*, which went on to become an American classic.[38]

So even when you think you can't make a difference in someone's life, remember the power of your words. Let encouragement bubble out of your mouth, giving hope to the disheartened and comfort to the distraught. Be sunshine to a darkened soul.

> *Heavenly Father, help me to remember that even when I feel like I don't have a lot to offer, I do have the power to refresh the people in my life. Give me encouraging words to share with those who are discouraged or disheartened. In Jesus' name. Amen.*

DAY 1

Lipstick Lesson

1. What is your reaction to the story of the woman on the stretcher and her lipstick? What does lipstick do for you, if anything?

2. Our words can be even more uplifting than lipstick! Look up the following verses and write about the positive effects of our lips.

   a. Proverbs 12:14

   b. Proverbs 15:23

   c. Proverbs 18:4

   d. Proverbs 18:20

   e. Proverbs 18:21

3. What key lesson did you learn today?

4. Write out our memory verse for this week: "A word fitly spoken is like apples of gold in a setting of silver" (Proverbs 25:11). To help you memorize this passage, write it out in the space below.

Meaningful Makeover

Today picture your mouth as a fountain of life. Purposefully look for opportunities to refresh and energize others. Journal about your words and the difference they make.

STEP 8

Opportunity

So then, as we have opportunity, let us do good to everyone, and especially to those who are of the household of faith.
Galatians 6:10

"Does anyone know what today is?" my husband asked the group of kids who had come up to the front of the church for the children's sermon.

Several kids shouted, "Father's Day!"

"Since it's Father's Day, would anyone like to say something nice about his dad?" John asked.

Silence.

"How about you, young man?" John pointed the microphone at a blond-haired boy. "Would you like to say one nice thing about your dad?"

The boy leaned into the microphone and said, "One nice thing about my dad."

Not exactly what my husband was looking for.

My husband gave this young man a chance to use his words to build up his father—to make his day. The boy missed an important opportunity. Fortunately, everyone laughed and his words were a source of humor.

However, when opportunities to express love or encouragement are neglected, the result is often disappointment or sadness. I recently read a story about a funeral. The minister conducting the funeral stayed at the graveside while the mourning husband stood at his wife's casket. Everyone else had left long ago, but the husband remained. Finally, the minister told the man he really should go home and rest.

The man refused to leave. "You don't understand," he told the other man. "I loved my wife."

"I can see that you loved her," the minister said.

"You don't understand," the man insisted. "I loved my wife."

"I am sure that you did. But it's time to go now."

"You don't understand," the husband repeated. "I loved my wife and once—I almost told her."[39]

How heartbreaking to know that wife never heard those important words—

words she most likely longed to hear. How sad to think the husband will have to live with the knowledge that he should have said them, that he could have said them—and didn't. Time ran out and the opportunity was lost.

A Word of Joy for Today

Christ's words to me in the Lord's Supper, "This is My body, this is My blood," communicate His sacrificial love for me.

Galatians 6:10 says, "So then, as we have opportunity, let us do good to everyone, and especially to those who are of the household of faith." The apostle Paul is urging us to take every chance we have to do good. Certainly, there are many ways to do good: work at a food pantry, volunteer at church, donate to missions. But one way we can all do good is with our words. Communicating grace to others doesn't require a fat bank account or a hefty amount of free time. We all have many opportunities to offer affirming words. Yet often we are stingy with them.

A big part of our Mouth Makeover has been to slough off the negative words from our lips—the sarcastic digs, the whining complaints, and persistent nagging. But just as important as taking off the negative shades of speech is remembering to put on the positive shades. Let's take every chance to speak loving words, healing words, life-giving words.

Share loving words. I just have to say it; my husband is very good at this. Unlike the grieving man in the story, my husband tells me every day of his love. He remembers all birthdays and anniversaries with lovely cards which include his own heartfelt expressions of devotion.

Don't miss the opportunity to speak loving words to the important people in your life. The widower lost his chance. We never know when time will run out for those we care about.

Fun Ways to Say I Love You

- Use lipstick to write "I love you" on the bathroom mirror for your husband.

- Invent a secret hand signal that means "I love you" to use with your kids when their friends are around.

- Call your parents and thank them for specific things they have done for you.

- Fill a jar with slips of paper that tell exactly what you love about your friend, and give the jar to her.

- Send a card to someone when he or she least expects it.

Speak healing words. I know one woman who periodically gets offended by a minor offense and subsequently refuses to speak a word—any word—to the person who upset her. Her silence may last for months or even years.

Life is too short for bitterness. Instead of withholding healing words, strive to be the first to offer words of mercy. Forgiveness will not only restore the relationship, but heal the pain of resentment in your own heart.

Communicate life-giving words. My friend Linda is exceptionally talented at sharing encouragement. I'm always amazed at how much better I feel about myself after a lunch date with Linda. I'm not really sure how she does it, but I'm studying her method so I can offer the same kind of uplifting words to the other people in my life.

Sometimes I neglect wearing positive shades of speech because I'm too focused on myself. I'm looking for a pat on the back. I'm hoping to hear an "atta girl" instead of looking for opportunities to say the same to someone else.

But since I started my Mouth Makeover, I've been trying to change. Now when I meet a friend or attend a meeting, I tell myself to look for opportunities to share an encouraging word. I notice my friend has a new scarf and I tell her she looks fabulous. The president of the organization does a tremendous job in leading the meeting and I make sure I communicate that fact before I leave. It doesn't take long and it doesn't cost me anything, but it may make a small improvement in someone's day.

✝ *Every moment that passes is an opportunity to share loving, healing, and life-giving words. Don't let time run out.*

Yes, I know. Some days it's very hard to do this. There are times when problems pile up at your feet and despair looms over your head in thick dark clouds. You truly are the one who needs a kind word. You don't feel like you have any to give. However, it just so happens that the best thing to do when you are discouraged is to find someone else who needs a lift. Because an interesting thing happens when we share uplifting words—our own hearts are lightened.

As you have opportunity, communicate messages of love and healing. Every chance you get, give life-giving words. Sharing grace won't drain your bank account. Saying "one nice thing" won't rob you of precious hours. Take every opportunity to speak love to the important people in your life. You never know when it will be too late.

STEP 8

> *Holy Spirit, forgive me for the times when I have been stingy with affirming words. Help me take every opportunity You offer to share loving and healing messages. Open my eyes to see those people who are in need of a kind word today. Don't let me miss a chance to speak grace. In Jesus' name. Amen.*

DAY 2

Lipstick Lesson

1. Today, make sure you say "one nice thing" to someone special in your life. If you are doing this study in a small group, use this opportunity to have each person say "one nice thing" about each member of the group. In the space below, make notes about what you might say.

2. Do you have any other fun ways to say "I love you"? Share them here and with your group.

3. Read Luke 6:27–38.

   a. Write down some of the specific ways this passage tells us to demonstrate love.

   b. Verse 31 says, "Do to others as you would have them do to you" (NIV). Write some words you would love to hear from others and make a point of saying them to someone else today!

   c. What does this passage say about forgiving others?

   d. According to verse 38, how can we receive more mercy and love?

199

4. What key lesson did you learn today?

5. Write out our memory verse for this week: "A word fitly spoken is like apples of gold in a setting of silver" (Proverbs 25:11). Read a phrase, then cover it and write it. Recite as much of the verse as you can without looking.

Meaningful Makeover

Choose one of the fun ways to say "I love you" on page 196 to complete today. Journal about the other person's reaction.

Powerful Prayer

I thank my God in all my remembrance of you, always in every prayer of mine for you all making my prayer with joy. Philippians 1:3–4

I first learned the power of intercessory prayer at Camp Luther. It all began at a worship service during a youth retreat. Guitar music filled the space as I sang along with other teens. Together, we laughed and cried as we talked about what God had taught us during the retreat.

At the end of the service, the camp director asked for prayer requests. A woman I didn't recognize spoke up. "Thanks for letting me join your group tonight. I'm staying in one of the camp cabins for the week," she said. "I would really appreciate your prayers for my eight-year-old nephew. He has just been diagnosed with a brain tumor. The doctors say there is nothing they can do for him."

Stillness hovered in the room as we all contemplated the heartbreak of a little kid dying of a brain tumor. The director prayed aloud and our hearts pled with God for healing.

The retreat ended the next day, and we all went home. Sorry to say, I didn't think much more about the sad story. Because the woman who asked for prayer wasn't part of our church, I never expected to hear any more about her nephew.

However, a few weeks later, one of the adult leaders of the youth group approached me. "I have some news," she said. "Remember the eight-year-old boy we prayed for at the youth retreat? The one with the brain tumor?"

I nodded.

"The tumor is gone! The doctors did more x-rays to see how much it had grown and it had completely disappeared! God answered our prayers!"

✝ *Praying for others is a powerful way to use our words.*

God is amazing. His power is astounding. Perhaps what is even more incredible is that He allows us to talk to Him in prayer. In fact, one of the best ways we can impact our world with our words is through prayer. The most meaningful way we can help our friends and family is to pray for them.

In several of his epistles, Paul recorded his prayers for the people receiving the letters. One such prayer is found in Philippians 1:3–11. Let's look at this prayer as a model of how to pray for our loved ones.

The prayer begins with a word of gratitude: "I thank my God in all my remembrance of you" (Philippians 1:3). How often do you remember to thank God for the people in your life? I admit that I often neglect this kind of prayer. But life would be so very different without my loving husband or wonderful children. My time on earth would be less rich without the treasure of friends. From now on, I will thank God whenever He brings them to mind.

Paul continues with a prayer for their work and their purpose: "Always in every prayer of mine for you all making my prayer with joy, because of your partnership in the gospel from the first day until now. And I am sure of this, that He who began a good work in you will bring it to completion at the day of Jesus Christ" (Philippians 1:4–6). We aren't all missionaries like Paul, but we are all partners in the Gospel. We all have a purpose in God's kingdom.

A Word of Joy for Today

My heavenly Father has given me the priceless privilege of coming to Him in prayer.

When our reason for living seems fuzzy, we can become discouraged. My friend, Gail, and I both went through a period of time when we struggled with our purpose. Our children were growing up and we wondered what our new roles would be now that we were transitioning from the role of active parent. During our regular coffee sessions, we shared prayer requests, often asking for wisdom and guidance for each other. Knowing that Gail was praying for me gave me patience and strength as I waited for God to reveal what He had in mind for me.

Finally, Paul prays for the spiritual life of his friends. When family members or friends are experiencing health problems, I include those on my prayer list. But even more important is their spiritual health. Paul continues:

> And it is my prayer that your love may abound more and
> more, with knowledge and all discernment, so that you may
> approve what is excellent, and so be pure and blameless for
> the day of Christ, filled with the fruit of righteousness that
> comes through Jesus Christ, to the glory and praise of God.
> (Philippians 1:9–11)

Following Paul's example, may we pray that our friends have the discernment to make wise decisions. Let's ask God to keep them pure in this messy world. And pray that they stay close to Jesus, honoring Him in all they do.

Praying Scripture

One way to pray for others is to use God's own words from the Bible. Below are some passages helpful in praying for loved ones.

Pray for their:

- health   3 John 1:2
- faith   Proverbs 3:5–6
- fears   Isaiah 41:10
- work   Psalm 90:17
- safety   Isaiah 43:2

God has chosen to work in response to our prayers. Let's use this potent word tool to impact our world. Remember your friends in prayer. Pray with joy.

Father in heaven, thank You for the privilege of prayer. It is so amazing that I can come to You any time of day and express my concerns. Lord, help me not to neglect this blessing. I want to be a prayer conduit for my world. In Jesus' name. Amen.

DAY 3

Lipstick Lesson

1. Tell about a time when the prayers of others meant a lot to you.

When I was pregnant — I See
Surgery in Branson

STEP 8

2. A few years ago, I discovered a specific way to pray Scripture that is particularly meaningful. Martin Luther outlined this method in his little book, *A Simple Way to Pray*, which he wrote in response to his barber's question on how to pray. In this little volume, Luther told how he prayed through the Ten Commandments, turning each into a word of instruction, a prayer of thanksgiving, a confession, and a petition. Read Philippians 1:3–11 and my examples of this method. Then read Ephesians 1:15–23 and write your own prayers using this "simple way to pray."

3. What key lesson did you learn today?

	Philippians 1:3–11	Ephesians 1:15–21
Instruction	Lord, You *instruct* me in Your Word to pray for the people in my life.	
Thanksgiving	Lord, I *thank* You that You complete the work that You begin in our lives.	
Confession	Lord, I *confess* that I sometimes neglect spending time in intercession for others.	
Petition	Lord, I make a *petition* for my loved ones, that You would give them knowledge and insight to choose what is best.	

4. Write out this week's memory verse. Try not to peek!

Meaningful Makeover

Is there someone in your life who could really use your prayers right now? In the space below or in your journal, personalize one of Paul's prayers from Question 2 on the preceding page, or ask God to give you a special Scripture verse to guide your prayers.

STEP 8

DAY 4

Mouth Mission

But the LORD said to me, "Do not say, 'I am only a youth'; for to all to whom I send you, you shall go, and whatever I command you, you shall speak." Jeremiah 1:7

"Your mission, should you choose to accept it, is . . ."

Every episode of the television show *Mission Impossible* opened with Jim Phelps hearing these words on a tape player right before the tape fizzled in a puff of smoke. Secret agent Phelps accepted his mission and dropped whatever he was doing to accomplish it. The life of an Impossible Missions Force agent was not his own. He had to sacrifice his own agenda in order to follow specific instructions to carry out a more important plan.

We are also on a mission—a mission to speak God's words of love and grace to a lost and discouraged world. In order to be an agent on this mission, sacrifice will be necessary. We will need to realize that our mouths are no longer ours to do with as we please. They now belong to God.

The Old Testament records the story of a man who received a mission from God. The Lord did not speak to Jeremiah on a self-destructing magnetic tape, but He clearly communicated a mouth mission for this man. The instructions for the mission began with a word of encouragement, "Before I formed you in the womb I knew you, and before you were born I consecrated you; I appointed you a prophet to the nations" (Jeremiah 1:5). God had a special mission in mind for Jeremiah even before he was born. He had hand-selected this man for the unique role of speaking God's words.

✝ *God has given each of us a unique mission to speak His words of love and grace to a lost and discouraged world.*

God has also chosen you and me for a particular assignment. He has placed each one of us in a strategic place in time and space to be able to use our words to bring others closer to Him. You don't believe me? Consider the words of Ephesians 2:10: "For we are His workmanship, created in Christ Jesus for good works, which God prepared beforehand, that we should walk in them." Our heavenly Father made you in a special way so you could carry out a unique part of His plan.

We may not feel up to the task. Jeremiah didn't either. He told the Lord, "I do not know how to speak, for I am only a youth" (Jeremiah 1:6). Jeremiah felt his words were not nearly good enough to qualify him to be God's spokesman. Perhaps this is the best place to begin a mission for God. When I recognize I am not able to accomplish it on my own, I will rely on God. If I admit I don't have the right words, I am open to receiving them from the Holy Spirit.

A Word of Joy for Today
God has uniquely created me for a divine purpose and plan.

But God tells Jeremiah not to put himself down. "Do not say, 'I am only a youth'" (Jeremiah 1:7a). Don't diminish your value. Don't think you can't complete God's assignment. The important things are trust in the Lord and the willingness to obey Him. God told Jeremiah, "For to all to whom I send you, you shall go, and whatever I command you, you shall speak. Do not be afraid of them, for I am with you to deliver you" (Jeremiah 1:7b–8a). On Mission Impossible, Mr. Phelps always accepted his mission. The show would have ended quickly if he had walked away from the smoldering tape deck and refused to follow instructions. The Book of Jeremiah would not have been written if the prophet had refused his mission. We cannot accomplish God's purpose in our lives if we are not willing to obey.

God may not call you to be a prophet like Jeremiah, but He may choose you to be the one to send a card of hope to a hurting friend. The Lord may not send you on a mission to Africa, but He may urge you to walk across the room to cheer up someone in your study group. The Father may not ask you to lead a Bible study, but He may bring to mind a friend who needs an encouraging phone call. Are you willing to accept the mission?

The Lord then touched Jeremiah's mouth and said, "Behold, I have put My words in your mouth" (Jeremiah 1:9b). God made Jeremiah's mission easier by giving him the right words to say. God will also help us to choose the right message for a grieving friend or a discouraged child. As we learn to pause and pray before we speak, we will tune our ears to the Holy Spirit's voice. He will help us accomplish our mission.

Mission Possible

Is God calling you to one of these assignments?

- Send daily, short, but encouraging e-mails to a friend who is going through a dark time.

- Tell a salesperson's supervisor about the excellent service you received.

- Send a friend a note saying you are praying for him or her—be sure to follow through!

- Stock up on some funny cards. Send one whenever you know someone who needs a laugh.

- Invite a neighbor who may not know Christ over for coffee.

Our words have a purpose. God told Jeremiah that he was appointed "to pluck up and to break down, to destroy and to overthrow, to build and to plant" (Jeremiah 1:10b). As we learned in Week 4, sometimes we are called on to speak the truth in love. We may need to uproot sinful behavior or destroy destructive attitudes. But we tear down in order to build. Our words have the power to plant joy and hope. Our mouths can build confidence and courage.

Dear friends, your mission, should you choose to accept it, is to speak God's grace to the people who cross your path. He has placed you at this particular crossroads of time and space to build up the people around you. Perhaps you are like the senior citizen my husband visited, doubting your purpose, or maybe you are a stay-at-home mom who feels her mission has been reduced to changing diapers and mopping up spills. Wherever you are, you have been chosen to speak God's words of love and grace. As you surrender your mouth as an instrument for God's purpose, He will give you the right words to carry out your assignment. Listen for the Holy Spirit's instructions—you are on a mission.

Almighty God, I am amazed that You have chosen me to be a part of Your plan. Open my eyes today to show me someone who needs a word of love or mercy. Give me the right words and the courage to share them. Thank You for allowing me to be an instrument of Your love. In Jesus' name. Amen.

DAY 4

Lipstick Lesson

1. How do you feel about being on a mission? Do you think it is possible or impossible?

2. Exodus tells another story about a man who didn't think he could speak for God. In Exodus 3, Moses meets God in a burning bush and receives his assignment to tell Pharaoh to let God's people go. Read Exodus 3–4:17.

a. What are some of Moses' objections to the mission (3:11 and 13; 4:1 and 10)?

b. Which objection do you most relate to?

c. How does God respond to Moses' objections?

d. Why do you think God got angry in 4:14?

e. According to 4:11–12, why are we able to accomplish our mouth mission even if we feel inadequate?

3. What key lesson did you learn today?

4. Write out this week's memory verse. Try not to peek!

Meaningful Makeover

On a 3 × 5 card, write the words *Mission Possible*. Underneath add these words from Jeremiah 1:7: "For to all to whom I send you, you shall go, and whatever I command you, you shall speak." Post the card in a prominent place to remind you of God's mission for your mouth. Journal about how the idea of a mission changed your words today.

STEP 8

DAY 5

Grace Glasses

STEP 8

And He said to her, "Your sins are forgiven." Luke 7:48

You are giving a dinner party. You scurry around making last-minute preparations. Check the stew. Light the candles. Cue the music. The most influential people in town will be arriving soon, and you want them to be impressed.

To ensure that your party will be talked about for weeks, you have invited a new resident who has been a hot topic ever since he began speaking around town. Some people totally disagree with his political views, but others are intrigued by him.

The doorbell rings and the guests arrive. Somehow they all seem to come at the same time and you wonder if you have greeted everyone appropriately, but right now, you are more concerned with getting the food served.

Everyone is enjoying the meal when a woman bursts into the house, weeping and crying. You've seen this woman before, but where? Oh, yes, she's been in the news lately. Although her makeup is now streaked, you can see she is the same woman who was arrested for soliciting at the mall.

Before you can stop her, the woman flings herself at your honored guest—the newcomer in town. You are simply appalled. She is at his feet—weeping and sobbing. What to do? Certainly your guest knows who this is and yet he doesn't seem bothered by her at all. He is looking at her with—how to describe it? Compassion? Love? Could he love her?

The guest of honor suddenly leans over to you and says, "I need to talk to you." You both get up and take a few steps away from the other guests, leaving the weeping woman crumpled on the floor. You assume he is going to ask you to get rid of this uninvited guest, but instead he tells you a story about two men who owe money to a notorious loan shark. One man owes $4,000 but the other is indebted to the tune of $40,000. Neither man has the money, but the loan shark decides to let them both off the hook. Then your guest asks you a seemingly stupid question, "Which man do you think will love the lender more?"

You give the obvious answer: "The one who owed $40,000, of course."

"You're right," your guest says and points at the woman on the floor. "You see this woman. We both know who she is. But she's sorry for what she's done.

That much is clear. She's been changed by my message of forgiveness and her appreciation is very apparent. Someone who feels they don't need forgiveness perhaps will not be as exuberant in their thanksgiving. You have invited me into your home, but you didn't make me feel welcome. She made me feel loved."

Your guest returns to the weeping woman. He takes her by the hand, helps her to her feet and says, "It's all right. You are forgiven. I can see your faith. You can now live in peace with God."

What would you say if you were confronted with this situation? In rereading the story of the sinful woman anointing Jesus (Luke 7:36–50), I was struck by the contrasting attitudes of Simon, the host of the dinner, and Jesus, the honored guest.

Simon saw only the woman's less-than-pristine reputation and immediately began judging her. Jesus saw the woman's repentant heart and immediately offered forgiveness. Jesus saw the woman through lens of grace.

Too often, I am more like Simon, looking only at a person's façade. I am concerned with surface issues. This attention to the external is also what led me to begin my Mouth Makeover. I was tired of embarrassing myself with my verbal faux pas. I thought I could improve my words by simply following a list of what to say and what not to say. My checklist included: Don't talk about people behind their back. Be polite. Don't swear. Say one nice thing to my husband today. (Just one; he'd better not expect any more!)

But I don't think Jesus used a checklist. I don't think He started out each day with a to-do list that read: Confront some Pharisees today. Preach the Gospel. Give Peter some encouragement. Instead, Jesus went through life noticing people. He looked into their hearts and used His words to meet their needs.

A Word of Joy for Today

Jesus sees beyond our failures. He peers inside repentant hearts and offers grace.

When Jesus peered into the soul of the "sinful woman," He saw a repentant and loving heart behind the corrupt reputation. He didn't give her a three-point lecture on how to improve her life. Jesus gave her the words she most needed to hear, "Your sins are forgiven."

✝ *A true Mouth Makeover is more than a list of what to say and what not to say; it is detecting the needs of the people in your life and offering God's grace.*

I want to be like Jesus and notice the people who need a word of forgiveness or a message of kindness. I want to offer more than overused clichés and empty platitudes. I want to avoid snap judgments and learn the story behind the story. I want to do more than follow a list of what to say and what not to say. I want to offer grace.

We have come to the end of this Mouth Makeover. Of course, this does not mean that we will cease struggling with our lips. In fact, if you meet me some day, and I say something stupid, I hope you won't think, "and she wrote a book about that!" I am certain to mess up and mess up often. Would you offer me some grace? I'll do the same for you.

Let's go through life with our new makeup bag stocked with the balm of encouragement, the lip plumper of praise, and the lip liner of truthfulness. Let's be ready to choose the shade of grace, the lip gloss of thankfulness, and the lip sealer of discretion. The Holy Spirit will teach us when each of these tools is needed.

Most of all, detect the people in your life who need a little compassion. Notice those who are desperate for some hope. Look behind outward appearances and offer mercy. Ask the heavenly Father for "grace glasses."

Precious Savior, thank You for looking into my heart and offering me grace. Give me eyes to see those who need a bit of hope or a message of mercy. Continue to make over my mouth to be a tool for Your glory. In Your name I pray. Amen.

DAY 5

Lipstick Lesson

1. Discuss what you have discovered about a Mouth Makeover through this book. What is the most important lesson you have learned?

2. Look back to the assessment you took on Week 1, Day 2 (p. 19). What unattractive mouth shades did you check? Now that we have come to the end of our Mouth Makeover, do you see any improvement in those areas?

3. LIP Study

Read the story of the sinful woman in Luke 7:36–50 and use the three-step LIP process to learn more about speaking grace. Read through the passage three times and follow these steps (I have done a few for you as examples):

Look for the Facts

Interpret the Meaning

Pursue the Application

Look for the facts. Don't make any interpretations here. Simply write what is happening in each verse.

Verse 36	Jesus went to the home of a Pharisee for dinner.
Verse 37	A woman who had led a sinful life came to the home, bringing an alabaster jar of perfume.
Verse 38	She wet His feet with her tears and wiped them with her hair. She kissed them and poured perfume on them.
Verse 39	The Pharisee knew this woman was a sinner and was appalled that Jesus would let her touch Him.
Verse 40	Jesus told Simon He had something to say.
Verse 41	
Verse 42	
Verse 43	
Verse 44	
Verse 45	

Verse 46

Verse 47

Verse 48

Verse 49

Verse 50

Interpret the meaning. Turn the lesson in the passage into a scriptural principle.

Verse 36   Jesus had fellowship with people even if He did not agree with them.

Verse 37   People desperate for mercy seek Jesus out.

Verse 38   Extravagant grace requires an extravagant response.

Verse 39   Those who have not accepted grace are often judgmental of others.

Verse 40   Jesus wants to speak to us.

Verse 41

Verse 42

Verse 43

Verse 44

Verse 45

Verse 46

Verse 47

Verse 48

Verse 49

Verse 50

Pursue the application. Turn the principle you discovered into a personal question that applies the truth to your life.

Verse 36   Do I tend to associate with only the people I agree with?

Verse 37   Do I seek out Jesus?

Verse 38   What is my response to Jesus' grace? Has it been extravagant or restrained?

Verse 39   Do I tend to be judgmental or merciful?

Verse 40   Am I ready to listen to what Jesus has to say to me? Verse 41

Verse 42

Verse 43

Verse 44

Verse 45

Verse 46 Verse 47

Verse 48

Verse 49

Verse 50

4. What key lesson did you learn today?

5. Write Proverbs 25:11 from memory.

Meaningful Makeover

Choose one question from those you posed in "Pursue the Application." Answer it honestly and come up with an action you can do to grow in that area.

Parting Thoughts

The most important words we can ever say are "I believe in Jesus Christ, the Son of God, as my Lord and Savior." These words are the foundation of a personal relationship with God. God loves you and has a plan for you to know Him and His mercy through His Son. He outlines this plan in His Word.

"For all have sinned and fall short of the glory of God" (Romans 3:23). No one is perfect. Everyone fails to meet God's standard of sinlessness. This sin prevents us from coming to Him and from entering heaven.

"For God so loved the world, that He gave His only Son, that whoever believes in Him should not perish but have eternal life" (John 3:16). Despite our sin, God loved us so much that He sent His own Son to take the punishment we deserved for our sins and mistakes. Jesus' death enables us to live with God—forever.

"For by grace you have been saved through faith. And this is not your own doing; it is the gift of God" (Ephesians 2:8). God gives us faith to believe in Jesus; we can't believe on our own. His grace and mercy save us from death.

"But to all who did receive Him, who believed in His name, He gave the right to become children of God" (John 1:12). By receiving Jesus in the water and Word of Holy Baptism, we become part of God's family.

I invite you to pray this prayer to the God who loves you and wants you to be part of His family:

Father in heaven, I realize that I am a sinner and fall short of what You want for my life. I know that I cannot save myself or earn eternal life. Thank You for sending Your Son, Jesus, to die for me. Through the power of His resurrection, You make me alive eternally. Help me to turn from my sins and follow You. Thank You that although I may still fail, You will forgive me because Jesus paid the price for my sins. Thank You for Your gift of faith in Jesus, my Savior, and for the promise of eternal life with You. In Jesus' name I pray. Amen.

God speaks His words of love and grace to you. Through God's free gift of faith in Jesus, you now are part of God's family!

Answers

STEP 1, DAY 1

1. Answers will vary, but might include: Lipstick is like the words that come out of our mouths in that we have a choice about both. Lipstick and the words we speak can both affect our beauty. Lipstick is not like our words in that it is not as easy to change our words as it is to change our makeup. Wearing lipstick or changing the color of our lipstick affects only our superficial beauty, while changing the shade of our speech will change our spiritual beauty and improve our relationships with other people and our Savior.

2. a. Proverbs 16:23: A wise heart will guide a woman's speech, helping her to teach others. Matthew 12:33–37: The mouth speaks what is in the heart. If there is evil in the heart, evil words come out; if there is good in the heart, good words come out. **b.** Romans 3:23–24: We are justified—made right in God's sight—through God's grace and Christ's redemptive work. Ephesians 2:8: We are saved by grace, not by our own good deeds. **c.** Psalm 18:1–2: A rock is a symbol of strength—God is mighty. We cannot accomplish a Mouth Makeover on our own, but as we rely on God's strength, we can make significant changes. Psalm 103:2–4: God is giving and forgiving. Because of this, I can go to Him for forgiveness when my mouth messes up.

3., 4. Answers will vary.

STEP 1, DAY 2

1. Answers will vary.

2. a. The angels were in awe of God's holiness. Although they were sinless, they were aware of their inferiority compared to God. Seeing the sinless angels respond this way makes me repentant of my sometimes casual approach to God. **b.** Answers will vary, but may include a renewed sense of wonder in God's presence, a resolve to treat God with the utmost respect. **c.** Answers will vary. **d.** Answers will vary.

3., 4. Answers will vary.

STEP 1, DAY 3

1., 2. Answers will vary.

3. a. God extends forgiveness and love to all who call on Him. **b.** We receive forgiveness of all our sins through God's Son. **c.** If we confess our sins, God will forgive us and cleanse away our sin and unrighteousness. **d.** Answers will vary, but one way we can make real God's truth of forgiveness is to memorize verses like 1 John 1:9.

4., 5. Answers will vary.

STEP 1, DAY 4

1. Answers will vary.

2. He says, "Yes!" to God's call to be His ambassador. **3.** Answers will vary.

4. a. Some of the phrases David uses to plead for forgiveness include: "have mercy on me," "blot out my transgressions," "hide Your face from my sins," and "create in me a clean heart." The word pictures include cleansing, purging with hyssop (which was a purifying ritual in the Old Testament temple), and washing until white as snow. **b.** Once we have received God's forgiveness, we are "clean" and "whiter than snow." We have "joy and gladness." We are pure in God's eyes; He blots out our iniquities. **c.** After David has received the joy of forgiveness, he promises to use his tongue to teach others how to return to God, to sing of God's righteousness, and to declare praise.

5., 6. Answers will vary.

STEP 1, DAY 5

1. Answers will vary.

2. LIP Study: Answers will vary. Some possible responses follow. *Look for the Facts:* verse 6: The tongue can corrupt a person and set the whole course of a life on fire. Verse 7: All kinds of animals have been tamed by man. Verse 8: No man can tame the tongue. It is a "restless evil," "deadly poison." Verse 9: With the tongue, we can praise God. With it, we also curse people who are created in God's image. Verse 10: Our mouths should not be conduits of both blessing and cursing.

Interpret the Meaning: verse 6: Control the small things in life, like the tongue, and the big problems will be minimized. Verse 7: God has given men power over animals. Verse 8: We can't tame our tongues without God's grace and power. Be aware of the bitter pain the tongue can cause. Verse 9: If we bless God, we should also treat all of His children with respect. Verse 10: If we are made new in Christ, our words should reflect His character.

Pursue the Application: verse 6: What small step can I take today to control my tongue? Verse 7: Do I recognize the power of God in my life? Verse 8: Am I trying to tame my tongue on my own? Verse 9: How can I treat the people in my life with more respect? Verse 10: Would someone listening in on one of my conversations be able to tell that I am a Christian?

3., 4. Answers will vary.

STEP 2, DAY 1

1., 2. Answers will vary.

3. a. To insult is to show contempt for somebody. **b.** To malign is to criticize someone spitefully. **c.** To slur is to demean somebody. **d.** To disparage is to refer disapprovingly or contemptuously to somebody or something. **e.** To smear is to say bad things about somebody. A possible definition of slander might be to treat someone with contempt using demeaning and critical words.

4. a. Only people who do not slander or speak evil about their neighbors are worthy of being in God's presence. **b.** God will destroy those who secretly slander their neighbors. **c.** When we speak evil against others, we are judging them. But that is God's job, not ours.

5., 6. Answers will vary.

STEP 2, DAY 2

1., 2. Answers will vary.

3. a. The men were to go into the Promised Land to assess what the land was like and whether the people living in it were strong or weak. **b.** The spies told the Israelites that although the land was good, they could not take it because the people living there were too big and powerful. **c.** The people refused to go into the Promised Land. They even talked about going back to Egypt. God sentences them to forty years of wandering in the wilderness. **d.** The discouragers died by a plague. **e.** Joshua and Caleb encouraged the people because they knew that if the Lord was with them, it did not matter how big the people were. **f.** Answers will vary but might include the observation that God rewarded the encouragers and punished the discouragers. Also, we must recognize that the power of our discouraging words might keep others from following God's will for their lives.

4., 5. Answers will vary.

STEP 2, DAY 3

1. Answers will vary.

2. a. Peter may have been discouraged, feeling like a failure. **b.** Peter's emotions may have included joy, happiness, and hope. **c.** Peter probably felt happy that at last he had done something right. He would have felt blessed that God had revealed the truth of Jesus to him. **d.** Jesus blesses Peter and speaks words of God's favor. Jesus tells Peter that he has been given privileged information. Jesus speaks encouraging words about Peter's future. **e.** We can remind others of God's blessings. We can encourage others by telling them that God has a special plan for their future.

3., 4. Answers will vary.

STEP 2, DAY 4

1. Answers will vary.

2. a. We are to pursue what is mutually edifying. **b.** We are to work at pleasing our neighbors and building them up. **c.** Paul tells us to "encourage the fainthearted."

3. a. To cheer is to shout encouragement or support or to make someone feel cheerful. **b.** To refresh is to renew someone's energy. **c.** To inspire is to stimulate someone to do something. **d.** To affirm is to declare support for something. **e.** To praise is to express admiration for somebody or something. To encourage is show support and build others up, to express admiration and spur them on to do great things.

4., 5. Answers will vary.

STEP 2, DAY 5

1. Answers will vary.

2. LIP Study: Answers will vary. Some possible responses follow. *Look for the Facts:* verse 41: When Elizabeth heard Mary's greeting, the baby leaped in her womb. Elizabeth was filled with the Holy Spirit. Verse 42: Elizabeth said in a loud voice, "Blessed are you among women. Blessed is the child you will bear." Verse 43: Elizabeth asked why she should be so favored—to have the mother of the Savior visit her. Verse 44: Elizabeth told Mary the effect her visit had on the baby. Verse 45: Elizabeth told Mary she would be blessed because she believed God's words.

Interpret the Meaning: verse 41: When you are the one giving encouragement, don't do it in your own power. Rely on the Holy Spirit to give you the right words. Verse 42: Speak God's blessing on others. Verse 43: Encouraging others puts the focus on them and not yourself. Verse 44: Tell others the positive effects they have had on your life. Verse 45: The most important encouragement is the encouragement of someone's faith and trust in God.

Pursue the Application: verse 41: Do I ask God to give me the right words of encouragement? Who is someone I know who could use some affirming words right now? Verse 42: Do I offer generic encouragement or do I speak God's blessing? Verse 43: Am I willing to focus on other people instead of myself? Verse 44: Do I tell others the positive effects they have had on my life? Verse 45: How can I encourage my family's faith? my friend's faith?

3., 4. Answers will vary.

STEP 3, DAY 1

1., 2. Answers will vary.

3. a. A person confident of his strength is likely to brag about it. **b.** David describes the mouth of the boaster as a sharp razor with a tongue that plots destruction and practices lying. **c.** The boaster trusted in his own riches rather than in God. If our confidence is in our own strength or financial success, we may feel the need to play that up in an effort to convince ourselves and everyone else of our power. **d.** David puts his trust in God's love instead of himself. He realizes that God is the One who works out good in his life and thanks Him for it. He waits for God instead of striving for himself. When we realize that all good things ultimately come from God, we are less likely to brag about them because we accept them as gifts. If we realize our own limited strength compared to God's power, we are less likely to boast about what we can do.

4., 5. Answers will vary.

STEP 3, DAY 2

1. Answers will vary.

2. Answers will vary but might include: "Honor one another above yourselves" (NIV) and "give preference to one another in honor" (NASB).

3. a. Honoring others will take hard work and perseverance. It will not come naturally. **b.** Jesus told his disciples, "as you did it to one of the least of these My brothers, you did it to Me" (Matthew 25:40). So when we are serving and honoring other people, we are also serving the Lord. **c.** Some of the ways we can show others honor are praying for others, giving to people in need, showing hospitality to others, blessing even those that revile us, and showing empathy to others. We are not to think ourselves above others and be too proud to associate with those who might not be as well off as we are. We need to be willing to forgive when we are wronged and let God take care of any inequities we may feel.

4., 5. Answers will vary.

STEP 3, DAY 3

1. Answers will vary.

2. a. Paul was a devout Jew. He was persecuted for Christ's sake, enduring imprisonments, beatings, shipwrecks, and danger. He had received a vision of heaven. **b.** When we realize our own weakness, we are more likely to rely on God's strength. **c.** Answers will vary. **d.** As humans, we will not come to God for His mercy if we think we can get to heaven on our own strength. It is only when we accept that we cannot do it on our own that we will accept God's grace, both for our salvation and for our continued spiritual growth.

4., 5. Answers will vary.

STEP 3, DAY 4

1., 2. Answers will vary.

3. a. God has unsearchable greatness. He is mighty, glorious, and majestic. God has abundant goodness and righteousness. He is gracious, merciful, slow to anger, abounding in steadfast love. He is good and merciful. He has dominion over an everlasting kingdom. The Lord is faithful and kind. He holds up all those who are falling. He is a provider to all and near to all who call on Him. The Lord is a listener—He hears our cries. **b.** Answers will vary.

4., 5. Answers will vary.

STEP 3, DAY 5

1. Answers will vary.

2. Answers will vary. LIP Study: Answers will vary. Some possible responses follow. *Look for the Facts:* verse 5: Jesus saw a large crowd approaching and asked Philip where they could buy bread for all the people. Verse 6: Jesus asked this question to test Philip. He already knew what He was going to do. Verse 7: Philip said that eight months of wages would not be enough to buy bread for the people. Verse 8: Andrew spoke up. Verse 9: Andrew told Jesus that there was a boy with five loaves of bread and two fish, but he knew that was not enough. Verse 10: Jesus had the people sit down There were about five thousand men. Verse 11: Jesus took the loaves, gave thanks, and gave everyone as much food as they wanted. Verse 12: When everyone had enough to eat, Jesus instructed the disciples to pick up the leftovers. Verse 13: They gathered twelve basketfuls of leftover pieces. Verse 14: After the people saw this miraculous sign, they began to say that surely this was the Prophet come into the world. Verse 15: Jesus knew they wanted to make Him king by force, so He withdrew by Himself.

Interpret the Meaning: verse 5: God may test our faith with impossible situations. He will direct our attention to see where He will act. Verse 6: God already has a miraculous plan for our most impossible situations. Verse 7: We tend to look at things in terms of money. Verse 8: Look around. There may be a part of the solution right under your nose. Verse 9: At first, the solution may not seem like enough. Verse 10: Our part is to obey: either to sit and wait or to serve. Verse 11: Give thanks to God for the solution He has in mind even before He has provided it. God abundantly supplies our needs. Verse 12: Be aware of God's working in your life. Verse 13: Notice the overabundance of God's provision. Verse 14: Recognize Jesus as God. In our thinking, we may limit Him—unaware of His miraculous ability to work in our lives. Verse 15: Don't seek the world's attention and status. Stay grounded by spending time alone with the Father.

Pursue the Application: verse 5: What is my "impossible situation" right now? Verse 6: Why do I panic when God already has the solution planned out? How can I learn to trust in God's ability to work everything out? Verse 7: Am I looking at my "impossible situation" through worldly eyes—thinking how much work or how much money it will take to fix it? Verse 8: Is God trying to show me a solution? Verse 9: Am I willing to trust that this solution will be adequate? Verse 10: Is God asking me to sit and wait? Or to serve? Am I willing to be obedient? Verse 11: Have I given thanks for God's solution even though I can't see it yet? Verse 12: Do I take note of God's provision? Verse 13: Could I keep a journal of God's care for me? Verse 14: Do I limit God? Do I look for a human-size remedy rather than a God-size rescue? Verse 15: How can I change my desire for worldly status to a pursuit of intimacy with God?

STEP 4, DAY 1

1., 2. Answers will vary.

3. a. They both lied about the amount of money they received for the land they sold. **b.** They both fell down and died. **c.** Answers may vary but may include: God displays His displeasure for lying in the Eighth Commandment, "Thou shalt not bear false witness against thy neighbor." **d.** Other people were selling property and giving all the money from the sales to the apostles. They may have felt pressure to do the same. **e.** Answers will vary.

4., 5. Answers will vary.

STEP 4, DAY 2

1. Answers will vary.

2. a. God sees me as wonderfully made. **b.** God sees me as beautiful and without flaws. **c.** God sees me as His own, as His creation. **d.** He sees me as precious and honored. **e.** He sees me as a loved child. **f.** Answers will vary.

3., 4. Answers will vary.

STEP 4, DAY 3

1. Answers will vary.

2. a. *Sincere* is defined as honest and open, free from hypocrisy. **b.** To be open is to be frank, completely free from concealment, accessible to all. **c.** *Transparent* is defined as free from pretence and deceit. **d.** To be candid is to be direct and frank.

3. a. Sincerity and honesty are valued. **b.** An honest answer is pleasant. **c.** It is not good to use flattery or masks to cover up greed. Live to please God; He can see your heart.

4., 5. Answers will vary.

STEP 4, DAY 4

1., 2. Answers will vary.

3. a. First, go to the brother alone. Second, if he doesn't listen, take one or two others along. Third, if he still refuses to listen, tell it to the church. Fourth, if he doesn't change, treat him as an unbeliever. **b.** Sometimes, it is the loving thing to do to confront someone. These steps attempt to gently bring the offender back. **c.** Answers will vary.

4., 5. Answers will vary.

STEP 4, DAY 5

1. Answers will vary.

2. a. A hypocrite is one who pretends to have virtues or qualities he does not have. **b.** Jesus said the Pharisees honored Him with their lips, but their hearts were far from God. **c.** Answers will vary, but might include: being fully present in worship, examination of hearts before worship, and asking God to help focus our hearts on Him.

3. LIP Study: Answers will vary. Some possible responses follow. *Look for the Facts:* verse 21: A quarrelsome man stirs up strife. Verse 22: Gossip is like choice morsels. Verse 23: Impassioned lips with an evil heart are like a glaze over pottery. Verse 24: A malicious man hides the deceit in his heart. Verse 25: Don't necessarily believe someone who is charming. Verse 26: Malice may be concealed by deception, but will eventually be exposed. Verse 27: If a man digs a pit, he will fall into it. Verse 28: "A lying tongue hates those it hurts."

Interpret the Meaning: verse 21: Don't keep the pot boiling. Verse 22: Gossip is like rich chocolate; it is enjoyed by many. Verse 23: Our mouths repeat what the heart feels. Verse 24: Deceit is like wearing a disguise or a costume. Verse 25: All of your inner alarms should sound when someone seems too charming. Verse 26: Truth comes out in the end. Verse 27: Eventually, you will suffer the consequences of deceit. Verse 28: Lies hurt other people.

Pursue the Application: verse 21: Do I stir up quarrels? Verse 22: Do I take pleasure in gossip? Verse 23: Do my words match my heart? Verse 24: How can I detect when someone is wearing a mask? Verse 25: Am I easily conned by charming talk? Verse 26: How would I feel if what is in my heart right now were exposed? Verse 27: Do my words reflect the truth? Verse 28: Do I use flattery in a bad way?

4., 5. Answers will vary.

STEP 5, DAY 1

1., 2. Answers will vary.

3. a. Answers given. b. Descriptive terms: tongues like swords, words like arrows. Examples of speech: criticism, put-downs. **c.** Descriptive terms: words like honeycomb. Examples of speech: encouraging and praising words. **d.** Descriptive terms: lips that speak knowledge are like rare jewels. Examples of speech: words that teach and inspire.

4., 5. Answers will vary.

STEP 5, DAY 2

1. Answers will vary.

2. a. Drop the matter; change the subject. **b.** Raise the other person's ego.

3. a. He who loves quarreling loves sin. **b.** It is honorable to avoid quarrels. A fool is quick to quarrel. **c.** Answers will vary.

4., 5. Answers will vary.

STEP 5, DAY 3

1., **2.** Answers will vary.

3. a. A quarrelsome wife is as annoying as a constant dripping. **b.** Better to live on the roof than with a quarrelsome woman. **c.** Better to live in a desert than with an ill-tempered wife. **d.** Answers will vary.

4., **5.** Answers will vary.

STEP 5, DAY 4

1., **2.** Answers will vary.

3. a. Second answer. **b.** Third answer. **c.** First answer. **d.** Third answer. **e.** Answers will vary, but may include: We don't have to be perfect to tell others about Jesus. We don't have to use big theological words. We don't have to travel far to be an evangelist. We can simply tell others about our experience with Jesus.

4., **5.** Answers will vary.

STEP 5, DAY 5

1. Answers will vary.

2. LIP Study: Answers will vary. Some possible responses follow. *Look for the Facts:* Colossians 3:16: Let God's Word dwell in you richly. Sing psalms and hymns with gratitude to God. 3:17: Whatever you do in word or deed, do it in Jesus' name, giving thanks. 4:2: Devote yourselves to prayer. 4:3: Pray that God will open a door for the message of Christ. 4:4: Pray that Paul would proclaim Christ clearly. 4:5: Be wise in the way you act toward outsiders. Make the most of every opportunity. 4:6: Use grace in your words.

Interpret the Meaning: Colossians 3:16: God's Word dwelling in us overflows in words of wise teaching and songs of praise. 3:17: Whatever we say, we should say it as representative of Jesus. 4:2: Devotion to prayer is an excellent way to use our words. 4:3: Prayer for those who share Christ is essential. 4:4: Pray for clear words when sharing Christ. 4:5: Be aware of opportunities to share Christ with those outside the faith. 4:6 Grace can help us spread the word.

Pursue the Application: Colossians 3:16: Does God's Word dwell in me and spill out in praise? 3:17: Do I view myself as an ambassador of Christ? 4:2: Am I devoted to prayer? 4:3: Am I praying for the mission work of others? 4:4: When I am speaking to non-Christians, do I pray for the right words? 4:5: Do I use the opportunities that are given me? 4:6: How can I remind myself to speak with grace in every conversation?

3., 4. Answers will vary.

STEP 6, DAY 1

1., 2., 3. Answers will vary.

4. a. The Israelites grumbled about their hardships and the food. **b.** Answers will vary. **c.** Fire burned the outskirts of the camp, God sent meat, but also a plague, and many died from the plague. **d.** He complained about being in charge of so many complainers. **e.** God eased the burden of leadership by instructing Moses to choose seventy elders to be appointed as leaders. **f.** Answers will vary, but might include: The people were complaining among themselves and, in effect, showing God disrespect. Moses took his complaint straight to God—to the One who could help.

5., 6. Answers will vary.

STEP 6, DAY 2

1. Answers will vary.

2. Psalm 6 Beginning: David feels faint; his soul is in agony. End: David knows God has heard his cry and all his enemies will be defeated. Psalm 22 Beginning: David feels God has forsaken him. End: David acknowledges God's dominion and talks of God's abundant provision. Psalm 64 Beginning: David asks God to hear his complaint and to protect him from his enemy. End: David rejoices in God's triumph over the enemy. Everyone will be talking about the wonderful things God has done. Psalm 69 Beginning: David feels like he is sinking fast. He is worn out from calling for help. End: David praises and thanks God in song.

3., 4. Answers will vary.

STEP 6, DAY 3

1., 2., 3., 4. Answers will vary.

STEP 6, DAY 4

1. Answers will vary.

2. a. God tells His people He doesn't need their animals. He desires the sacrifice of thank offerings. **b.** "The wicked" use their tongues for evil and deceit. They speak against others. **c.** They forgot God. If we forget that God sees everything, we may not act in a God-pleasing way. **d.** Answers will vary.

4., 5. Answers will vary.

STEP 6, DAY 5

1., 2. Answers will vary.

3. LIP Study: Answers will vary. Some possible responses follow. *Look for the Facts:* verse 3: You will joyfully draw water from the well of salvation. Verse 4: Give thanks to the Lord. Proclaim to the nations what He has done. Verse 5: Sing to the Lord because He has done glorious things. Verse 6: Shout and sing, because your God is great.

Interpret the Meaning: verse 3: Our joy comes from salvation. Verse 4: Because of our joy, we give thanks to the Lord and tell others what He has done for us. Verse 5: Because God has done glorious things for us, we will use music to tell the world of Him. Verse 6: God is great—so sing and shout!

Pursue the Application: verse 3: Do I feel joy today? If not, is it because I do not fully appreciate God's gift of salvation? Verse 4: Have I thanked God today? Have I told others what He has done? Verse 5: What glorious things has God done for me lately? Verse 6: Am I enthusiastic about what God has done for me?

4., 5. Answers will vary.

STEP 7, DAY 1

1., 2. Answers will vary.

3. a. We should hold back words that misuse God's name. **b.** We should avoid judgmental words. **c.** We should avoid gossiping or telling secrets. **d.** We should avoid godless chatter.

4., 5. Answers will vary.

STEP 7, DAY 2

1. Answers will vary.

2. a. We can explain why we are angry without berating the other person or purposely hurting him or her with our words. **b.** Take care of problems quickly. Keep short accounts. **c.** Answers will vary. **d.** Continuing to hold anger in your heart can allow bitterness to grow. Your anger may cause you to lash out at the person with whom you are angry, or even at other people in your life.

3., 4. Answers will vary.

STEP 7, DAY 3

1. Answers will vary.

2. a. Job's friends sat with him in silence. **b.** They told Job that he must have done something wrong. They thought that was the only explanation for all the tragedy in his life. **c.** Job told his friends, "If only you would be silent." **d.** Sometimes, the best way to help our friends is through our presence and not through our words.

3., 4. Answers will vary.

STEP 7, DAY 4

1., 2., 3., 4. Answers will vary.

STEP 7, DAY 5

1. Answers will vary.

2. LIP Study: Answers will vary. Some possible responses follow. *Look for the Facts:* verse 4: The Pharisees told Jesus, "This woman was caught in the act of adultery." Verse 5: Moses' Law commanded the punishment of stoning. They asked Jesus what He thought. Verse 6: The Pharisees were trying to trap Jesus. Jesus didn't answer; instead, He wrote in the dirt. Verse 7: Jesus said, "If any one is without sin, let him throw the first stone." Verse 8: He stooped down and wrote on the ground again. Verse 9: The Pharisees went away one at a time, the older ones first. Verse 10: Jesus asked the woman, "Has no one condemned you?" Verse 11: Jesus said He did not condemn her either, but told her to leave her life of sin.

Interpret the Meaning: verse 4: We should be more concerned with our own sin than with the sin of others. Verse 5: Adultery is a serious sin. Verse 6: Our words have consequences; it is good to pause before we speak. Verse 7: Because I am not perfect, I don't have the right to judge. Verse 8: Sometimes, silence is the best communication tool. Verse 9: When we truly look at our own lives, we realize we do not have the right to condemn others. Verse 10: Mercy trumps judgment. Verse 11: Jesus forgives sin, but He also wants us to repent and change our behavior.

Pursue the Application: verse 4: Am I more concerned with my sin or others' sins? Verse 5: Do I honor my marriage? Verse 6: Do I pause before I speak? Verse 7: How can looking at my own life help me not to judge others? Verse 8: Do I use silence in a good way? Verse 9: Do I sometimes wrongly assume I have the right to judge others? Verse 10: How can I show mercy without excusing sin? Verse 11: Can I be as forgiving as Jesus?

3., 4. Answers will vary.

STEP 8, DAY 1

1. Answers will vary.

2. a. Our words can bring blessings into our own lives. **b.** When you give a helpful word, you can bless others and bring joy to your life. **c.** Words of wisdom are refreshing like deep waters or bubbling brooks. **d.** A man who speaks wisely will reap a harvest from his words. **e.** Our tongues have the power to give life and refreshment to others.

3., 4. Answers will vary.

STEP 8, DAY 2

1., 2. Answers will vary.

3. a. Do good, even to those who hate you. Bless your enemies. Give without expecting anything in return. Don't judge; instead forgive. **b.** Answers will vary. **c.** We are not to judge or condemn others. If we forgive others, we will be forgiven. **d.** We can receive mercy and love by giving it to others.

4., 5. Answers will vary.

STEP 8, DAY 3

1., 2., 3., 4. Answers will vary.

STEP 8, DAY 4

1. Answers will vary.

2. a. Moses didn't think he was worthy. He didn't know God's name. He didn't think people would listen to him. Moses didn't think he was eloquent. **b.** Answers will vary. **c.** God patiently gave Moses solutions for every objection. He promised to be with Moses and gave him the ability to do miracles to display God's presence to others. **d.** God gave Moses a solution for every objection and still Moses did not want to speak for God. **e.** God is the maker of our mouths. He is able to help us speak.

3., 4. Answers will vary.
WE STEP EK 8, DAY 5

1., 2. Answers will vary.

3. LIP Study: Answers will vary. Some possible responses follow. *Look for the Facts:* verse 41: Two men owed money to a money lender. One owed about fifty days of wages, the other five hundred days. Verse 42: The moneylender canceled both debts. Jesus asked Simon which man would love the moneylender more. Verse 43: Simon said the one who was forgiven more. Jesus told Simon he was correct. Verse 44: Simon did not wash Jesus' feet, but the woman wet them with her tears and dried them with her hair. Verse 45: Simon did not greet Jesus with a kiss, but the woman continually kissed His feet. Verse 46: Simon did not put oil on Jesus' head, but the woman poured perfume on His feet. Verse 47: Jesus forgave the woman and she displayed her love for Him. Those who have been forgiven little, love little. Verse 48: Jesus told the woman that her sins were forgiven. Verse 49: The other guests wondered who Jesus was because He forgave sins. Verse 50: Jesus told the woman her faith had saved her.

Interpret the Meaning: verse 41: We all owe God a great debt. Verse 42: God cancels all of our debts because of Jesus. Verse 43: If we realize the enormity of the debt we owe, we will be more grateful when it is forgiven. Verse 44: Pride may keep us from exhibiting gratitude for forgiveness. Verse 45: True faith will be exhibited in acts of love. Verse 46: True faith will be shown in acts of sacrifice. Verse 47: Overflowing love is a proper response to God's forgiveness. Verse 48: God is the only One who can forgive sins. Verse 49: People often question who Jesus is. Verse 50: Only faith in Jesus can save.

Pursue the Application: verse 41: Do I realize the enormity of the debt of my sin? Verse 42: Do I acknowledge Jesus as my debt-payer? Verse 43: Do I show my gratitude to Jesus for my forgiveness? Verse 44: Am I too proud to be demonstrative in my gratitude? Verse 45: How can I show God my love? Verse 46: Am I ready to make sacrifices to demonstrate my gratitude for salvation? Verse 47: Do I exhibit overflowing love for God? Verse 48: Do I believe Jesus forgives sins? Verse 49: Do I let others know that Jesus is the only One who can forgive sins? Verse 50: Do I believe in Jesus and His forgiveness?

4., 5. Answers will vary.

ENDNOTES

1. Pallingston, Jessica, *Lipstick: A Celebration of the World's Favorite Cosmetic* (New York: St. Martin's Press, 1999), 2.

2. Jaynes, Sharon, *The Power of a Woman's Words* (Eugene, Oregon: Harvest House Publishers, 2007), 11.

3. Pegues, Deborah Smith, *30 Days to Taming Your Tongue* (Eugene, Oregon: Harvest House Publishers, 2005), 109.

4. Jaynes, 53.

5. Jaynes, 53.

6. Adapted from book by Stephanie Marston, *The Magic of Encouragement: Nurturing Your Child's Self-Esteem* (Pocket Books, 1992), 118–119.

7. Miller, Calvin. *The Power of Encouragement* (Wheaton, Illinois: Tyndale House Publishers, Inc. 2003), 5.

8. Miller, viii.

9. http://www.quotegarden.com/humility.html, accessed November 4, 2011.

10. Youssef, Michael, *Empowered by Praise: How God Responds When You Revel in His Glory* (Colorado Springs, Colorado: WaterBrook Press, 2002), 173.

11. http://www.allfamousquotes.net/bragging-quotes, accessed November 4, 2011.

12. http://www.blueletterbible.org/commentaries/comm_view.cfm?AuthorID=4&contentID=1672&commInfo=5&topic=John&ar=Jhn_6_3, accessed November 9, 2011.

13. Callaway, Phil, *To Be Perfectly Honest: One Man's Year of Almost Living Truthfully Could Change Your Life. No Lie.* (Colorado Springs, Colorado: Multnomah Books, 2011), 8.

14. Foster, Richard J., *Celebration of Discipline: The Path to Spiritual Growth* (San Francisco: HarperSanFrancisco, 1978, 1988, 1998), 157.

15. Kent, Carol and Karen Lee-Thorp, *Six Essentials of Spiritual Authenticity* (Colorado Spring, Colorado: NavPress, 2007), 50.

16. Kent, 52.

17. http://www.blueletterbible.org/lang/lexicon/lexicon.cfm?Strongs=G5485&t=KJV, accessed January 3, 2012.

18. Pegues, 33–34.

19. Ibid, 32.

20. http://www.blueletterbible.org/lang/lexicon/lexicon.cfm?Strongs=G5485&t=KJV, accessed January 3, 2012.

21. http://www.blueletterbible.org/lang/lexicon/lexicon.cfm?Strongs=G5485&t=KJV, accessed January 3, 2012.

22. http://quotationsbook.com/quote/7591/, accessed July 25, 2012.

23. Caryn Dahlstrand Rivadeneira, *Grumble Hallelujah: Learning to Love Your Life Even When It Lets You Down* (Carol Stream, Illinois: Tyndale House Publishers, 2011), 9.

24. This story, "What to Do with Toilet Seat Gifts," was originally published on Kyria.com. Used by permission of Christianity Today International, Carol Stream, IL 60188.

25. Bonhoeffer, Dietrich, *Letters and Papers from Prison* (Minneapolis: Fortress Press, 2009), xx–xxi.

26. http://en.wikipedia.org/wiki/Lip_gloss, accessed August 1, 2012.

27. Emmons, Robert A., http://gratitudepower.net/science.htm, accessed August 1, 2012.

28. Emmons, Robert A., http://gratitudepower.net/science.htm, accessed August 1, 2012.

29. http://thinkexist.com/quotation/i_would_maintain_that_thanks_are_the_highest_form/207966.html, accessed August 1, 2012.

30. Jaynes, 208.

31. *Noah Webster's First Edition of an American Dictionary of the English Language* (San Francisco California: foundation for American Christian Education, 1996).

32. http://www.brainyquote.com/quotes/quotes/a/ambrosebie104027.html, accessed July 25, 2012.

33. http://itre.cis.upenn.edu/~myl/languagelog/archives/003420.html, accessed February 3, 2012.

34. http://thinkexist.com/quotation/the_friend_who_can_be_silent_with_us_in_a_moment/209085.html, accessed February 3, 2012.

35. http://www.hebrew4christians.com/Meditations/Be_Still/be_still.html, accessed February 8, 2012.

36. http://thinkexist.com/quotations/silence/2.html. accessed February 9, 2012.

37. Pallingston, 67.

38. Jaynes, 83–84.

39. Story adapted from *Words That Hurt, Words that Heal: How to Choose Words Wisely and Well* by Joseph Telushkin (New York: William Morrow and Company, 1996), 154.